RUM

A TASTING COURSE

RUM

A TASTING COURSE

IAN BURRELL

CONTENTS

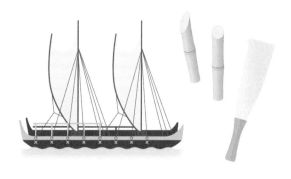

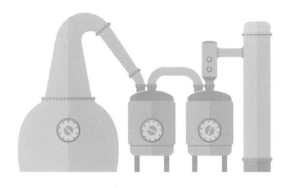

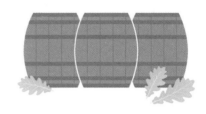

60 HOW IS RUM MADE?

94 TASTING RUM

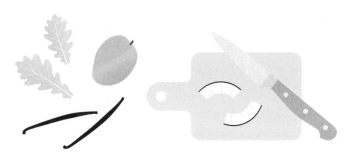

114 NAVIGATING RUM BY REGION

188 CLASSIC RUM COCKTAILS

A FLAVOUR-FOCUSED APPROACH

This book is all about the flavour of rum.

My main aim in this book is to help you celebrate and learn about the diverse and nuanced flavours that can be present in the sugarcane spirit we lovingly know as rum. You will discover that rum, like other alcoholic beverages such as whisky or wine, can have a wide range of flavour profiles.

They say that knowledge is power, but it's the use of knowledge that is truly powerful. My intention is to share with you a little of the rum knowledge that I have acquired over the years as a global rum ambassador, so that you can use it to help you on your journey as you travel the worldwide landscape of the rum category. You will discover that rum's diverse flavour profiles are influenced by factors such as the type of sugarcane used, the fermentation process, distillation methods, ageing conditions, and blending techniques.

My first official steps on the "rum road" actually took place when I was about four days old, according to my Jamaican mother. She told me that a little rum

MY INTENTION IS TO SHARE WITH YOU
A LITTLE OF THE RUM KNOWLEDGE
THAT I HAVE ACQUIRED OVER THE YEARS
AS A GLOBAL RUM AMBASSADOR.

was rubbed on my lips to help me to sleep. On reflection, that seemed to be a cultural practice passed on from generation to generation. Just like the rum category itself, rum styles – most of which you'll learn about in this book – are born, nurtured, matured, and then handed down to the present-day trustees.

If you're seeking to become a rum aficionado, you will also find in the following pages a little "tot" of rum's history. It's important to understand where the spirit has come from in relation to current interpretations. Many connoisseurs, experts, and ambassadors draw upon these historical stories when evaluating today's rums. And evaluating a rum is made even easier once you've learned to recognize aromas and flavours using the tools and techniques that I share.

Once you've identified your chosen rum, how do you best appreciate it? Neat is always a great way to establish a rum's true character, but drinking it with a mixer or in a cocktail has helped the spirit reach a wider audience. Many of the classic cocktail recipes in this book have stood the test of time, cementing rum's connection to tropical escapism. Cocktails are a fun way to explore rum's versatility, and, with the knowledge acquired in this book, will help you create the ultimate rum experience.

ABOUT THE RUMS IN THIS BOOK

The hardest thing about reviewing the 100 rums in this book is what to leave out, for each brand has an amazing story to tell and is not served justice by the small amount I have written about it.

To make things easier to navigate, I have grouped the rums by region, for rum is a global spirit made in all four corners of the world. For me, regionality is the best and easiest way to categorize rum. Each region has its rules, regulations, or guidelines that set it apart from its competitors. I have omitted rums that are spiced, flavoured, or heavily sweetened, as that is a separate style of rum best explained in another book.

I have included a brief flavour profile with each rum, which is a guide, but not gospel, to the rum's characteristics. Everyone has their own interpretation of aroma and flavour based on their experiences. There is no right or wrong flavour profile to rum – just the one that you taste and appreciate.

Cheers!

WHAT
IS
RUM?

OFTEN HAILED AS THE "SPIRIT OF THE CARIBBEAN", rum is an alcoholic beverage crafted from sugarcane byproducts, such as sugarcane juice, sugarcane syrup, or molasses. It undergoes fermentation, distillation, and sometimes an ageing process, resulting in a diverse range of flavours, from light and crisp to heavy and complex. With origins tracing back to the sugarcane plantations of the Caribbean, rum carries a rich history intertwined with the region's colonial past and cultural heritage. It embodies the essence of tropical climates, offering a taste of the tropics in every sip. Whether enjoyed neat, mixed in cocktails, or added to culinary creations, rum is a versatile and beloved libation cherished by enthusiasts worldwide for its warmth, depth, and storied tradition.

LEGAL DEFINITIONS OF RUM

There is no global definition or standard of identity for rum. But nor is there one for whisky, brandy, or even vodka. Like other spirits, rum has a long history and is produced in various regions around the world, each with its own traditions, methods, and cultural significance.

REGIONAL VARIATIONS

Diverse traditions and cultures have led to differences in how rum is made and perceived, making it challenging to establish a single set of rules that satisfies all producers and consumers. There is also considerable variation in the production methods used to make rum, including differences in raw materials, fermentation techniques, distillation processes, ageing methods, and blending practices. These variations result in a wide range of flavour profiles and characteristics, further complicating efforts to establish uniform standards.

THE CONSUMERS' CHOICE

Consumers have diverse tastes and preferences when it comes to rum, and what is considered desirable in one market may differ in another. In Jamaica, for instance, the biggest selling and most popular rum is unaged and bottled at 63% alcohol by volume (ABV). This product would be illegal to make and sell as rum in Venezuela, as all rums in that country, by law, must be aged for a minimum of two years and cannot be bottled at a strength higher than 50% ABV.

COMMON ELEMENTS

Although the legal definition of rum can vary depending on the country of origin or jurisdiction where it's sold, there are some common elements found in many legal definitions of rum.

RAW MATERIAL

Rum is typically defined as a distilled alcoholic beverage made from sugarcane byproducts, such as molasses or sugarcane juice. Some regions may have specific requirements regarding the source and quality of these raw materials.

ALCOHOL CONTENT

Legal definitions often specify the minimum and maximum alcohol by volume (ABV) allowed for a spirit to be classified as rum (see above right). This helps ensure consistency and quality across different products.

HOW MUCH ALCOHOL IS IN RUM?

Some countries specify the legal amount of alcohol that can be present in rum.

MEXICO 35% ABV

In Mexico, the legal minimum for rum is 35% ABV.

UK 37.5% ABV

Any rum sold in the UK must be at least 37.5% ABV.

US 40% ABV

In the United States, rum must be bottled at no less than 40% ABV.

57.15% ABV

Overproof rum is at least 57.15% ABV.

In Guatemala, all rums must be made from sugarcane syrup or "virgin cane honey", so officially, Guatemalan rums cannot be made from sugarcane juice or molasses. A global standard of identity would need to accommodate these varying preferences while ensuring transparency and authenticity.

Despite the absence of a global standard, there are efforts within the rum industry to promote best practices, quality assurance, and transparency through voluntary initiatives, industry associations, and regional certifications such as trademarks and geographical indicators (GIs).

CARICOM RUM STANDARD

The Caribbean Community (CARICOM) rum standard, established in 1991, applies to all 14 independent members of the Caribbean Community. It's a collective agreement endorsed by CARICOM governments and acts as the national standard for each member state. Jamaica has its own published standard, but it aligns with the CARICOM standard locally; its own standard applies only to rums exported outside the Caribbean. The Dominican Republic maintains its own unique standard.

PRODUCTION PROCESS

Legal definitions may outline the basic steps involved in rum production, such as fermentation, distillation, and ageing. They may also regulate aspects of the production process, such as the use of additives or flavourings, including sweeteners.

GEOGRAPHICAL INDICATION

In some cases, legal definitions of rum may include provisions related to a geographical indicator (GI), specifying that certain types of rum can only be produced in specific regions or countries known for their rum production.

LABELLING REQUIREMENTS

Regulations often govern how rum is labelled, including requirements for the disclosure of alcohol content, ageing duration, and any additives used in production. Labelling may also include information about the rum's origin or production methods (see pp92–93).

CULTURAL DEFINITIONS OF RUM

Legally, all rum *must* be made from sugarcane, but not all sugarcane spirits are rum. So when is a rum not a rum, but simply a sugarcane spirit?

SPIRITS AND DISTILLATES

The world's biggest selling gin, Ginebra San Miguel, is made from sugarcane, as well as some vodka and brandy. In India, even some whisky has a sugarcane spirit base. Therefore, just because a product is distilled from sugarcane, it should not be automatically classed as rum.

This is also true in regards to sugarcane distillates that have cultural and local definitions (see right). Cultural definitions of locally named sugarcane spirits are an important factor in ensuring that these historically named beverages are preserved, respected, and protected as they grow internationally. It would be inappropriate to categorize them as simply "rum" just because they are made from one of the many varieties of sugarcane.

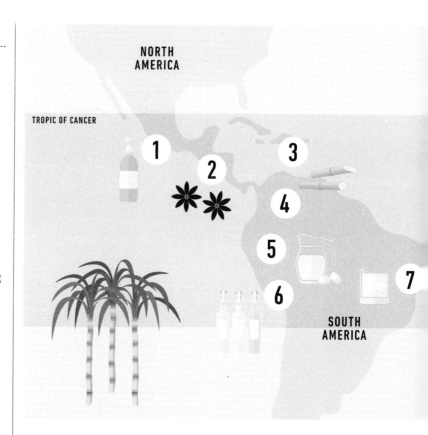

SUGARCANE SPIRITS AROUND THE WORLD

There are several sugarcane spirits from various parts of the world that, while similar to rum in production methods, may not be culturally referred to as rum.

JUST BECAUSE A PRODUCT IS DISTILLED FROM SUGARCANE, IT SHOULD NOT BE AUTOMATICALLY CLASSED AS RUM.

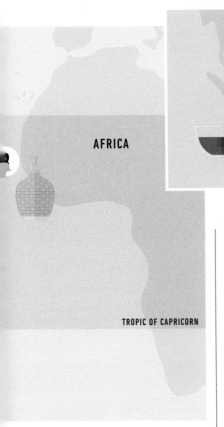

INDONESIA

9

AFRICA

TROPIC OF CAPRICORN

5. VICHE

Viche is a traditional African Colombian spirit made with sugarcane juice or molasses. It has varying flavour profiles across regions and has recently achieved geographical indicator (GI) status.

6. CAÑAZO

Cañazo is a Peruvian distilled spirit crafted from fermented sugarcane juice. With diverse flavours influenced by its production methods, it's central to Peruvian culture and prized for its social and medicinal roles.

7. CACHAÇA

Originating from Brazil, *cachaça* is a spirit made from sugarcane juice that is a key ingredient in the Caipirinha cocktail. While similar to rum in production, *cachaça* has its own distinct cultural identity.

8. GROGUE

Grogue is a traditional spirit from Cape Verde made from distilled sugarcane juice. Crafted in artisanal distilleries, it carries a unique flavour, often described as robust and earthy.

9. BATAVIA ARRACK

Originating from Indonesia, Batavia arrack is a distilled spirit made from sugarcane juice or molasses and fermented red rice. Used in cocktails, it has a unique, funky flavour profile with hints of fruit, spice, and earthiness.

2. AGUARDIENTE

Commonly found in Latin American countries, *aguardiente* is a strong distilled spirit made from sugarcane. It has various regional variations and may be flavoured with anise or other botanicals.

3. CLAIRIN

Hailing from Haiti, *clairin* is a traditional sugarcane spirit known for its artisanal production methods and diverse flavour profiles. It's often produced using wild yeast strains and small-scale distillation techniques.

4. AGUARDIENTE DE CAÑA

Similar to *aguardiente*, *aguardiente de caña* refers to sugarcane-based spirits made in Spanish-speaking countries, often with regional variations in production methods and flavour profiles, such as *aguardiente de caña* from Colombia and Central America.

I. CHARANDA

Originating from the Mexican state of Michoacán, *charanda* is a spirit made from sugarcane juice with protected designation of origin (PDO) status. It's often compared to rum due to its similar production process.

MOONSHINE

Prohibited sugarcane spirits, often referred to as moonshine, have deep cultural roots in many regions. This clandestine distilling produces potent but unregulated spirits.

A CULTURAL TRADITION

Prohibited sugarcane spirits are an integral part of local traditions, often associated with celebrations, rituals, and social gatherings. The production and consumption of these spirits are deeply ingrained in the community fabric, reflecting historical resistance to colonial and postcolonial regulations. While authorities seek to control moonshine for health and safety reasons, the allure of tradition and culture ensures their continued existence, perpetuating a complex relationship between legality, tradition, and cultural identity.

GUARO DE CONTRABANDO

Guaro de contrabando, which translates as "smuggled *guaro*", is a clear spirit made predominantly from sugarcane juice or sugarcane syrup in Central America.

CHIRRITE

Chirrite is a typical type of *guaro de contrabando* from Costa Rica. It's made in remote, hidden locations called *sacas de guaro* to avoid being discovered by the authorities.

BABASH

Babash is an extremely strong rum made from molasses and syrup, and is popular in Trinidad. Many Trinidadian bars have a plastic bottle of this "under-the-counter" rum, but risk being fined for selling it.

JOHN CROW BATTY

In Jamaica, John Crow Batty is as legendary as the country's music. Freshly distilled, undiluted alcohol is stolen from distilleries to be sold cheaply to locals and tourists. Extra strong and unrefined, it is normally between 85 and 90% ABV.

PITORRO

Pitorro is made in Puerto Rico and is much stronger than the local commercial rums. Production is ramped up around Christmas to use in popular drinks like the Coquito, made with rum, cream, condensed milk, coconut milk, and spices.

PROHIBITED SUGARCANE SPIRITS ARE AN INTEGRAL PART OF LOCAL TRADITIONS, OFTEN ASSOCIATED WITH CELEBRATIONS, RITUALS, AND SOCIAL GATHERINGS.

THARRA

Tharra is a *desi daru*, a countryside liquor made in rural areas of India and Pakistan. Like most rural spirits, it is very cheap to make, and distillation techniques have been passed down from generation to generation in local communities.

TILAMBIC

Made in Mauritius, this crude rum is illegally produced in the backyards of homes in small towns throughout the island. Fruits and spices are added to the spirit to mask the rough taste. This is called *rhum arrangé* (mixed or rearranged rum).

AKPETESHIE

Akpeteshie, meaning "in hiding", is a traditional distilled spirit from Ghana. Made from sugarcane juice (or palm wine), it is a potent liquor with a high alcohol content. Banned by British colonial authorities, it was legalized in 1962.

HAMMOND

Hammond is a homemade rum made in illicit stills in St Kitts and Nevis. Also known as "bush rum", it has been made for centuries by locals.

WA BIO

Wa bio, also known as mountain dew, is made in Dominica, usually in stills hidden in bushes in the remote countryside of the island. It is made from brown sugar, molasses, yeast, and water.

CATEGORIES OF RUM

In the early days of rum production, all rums were a transparent liquid and categorized by their place of origin. Later, rum started to become more varied as it was marketed to the consumer.

EARLY RUMS

Especially in the 17th century, all rums were water-white. But as the fiery sugarcane spirit began to be tamed by the use of wooden barrels, which imparted their golden colour, or the addition of burnt sugar (caramel), wines, or even fruits and spices, rum's presentation and categorization became more varied.

Some rums were sold as Jamaican rum or Demerara rum, for example. Or rum was sold as white rum or dark rum, usually for the same price, but with the dark rum coloured with rum caramel. Rum could even be flavoured with pineapples or accidentally "wood flavoured" as it travelled in barrels on ships across the ocean to thirsty European drinkers.

In recent times, the industry's need to classify or compartmentalize rum has led to many different labels being used to describe rums. Here are some examples of how rum is correctly, and sometimes misleadingly, categorized.

BY COUNTRY OF ORIGIN

Rum can be categorized by its country of origin. Like Scotch from Scotland and bourbon from the United States, countries such as Jamaica, Cuba, and Martinique have rum styles, characteristics, or a set of regulations that define what can or cannot be called rum in their respective countries.

BY FORMER COLONIES

Rum classification can reflect historical influences. British-style rums, notably from Jamaica and Barbados, are often robust and pot distilled. Spanish-influenced rums, like those from Cuba and the Dominican Republic, tend to be lighter bodied and made in column stills. French-style rums, including those from Martinique and Guadeloupe, emphasize *terroir* and *agricole* production methods. Portuguese-style rum is similar to French-influenced rums but uses sugarcane juice as opposed to molasses.

RUM CLASSIFICATION BY RAW MATERIAL HIGHLIGHTS DIVERSE PRODUCTION METHODS.

BY RAW MATERIAL

Rum classification by raw material highlights diverse production methods. Molasses-based rums, or traditional rums, are common worldwide and offer richness and depth. *Rhum agricole*, or agricultural rum, is crafted from sugarcane juice and presents grassy and vegetal notes.

BY DISTILLATION

Recently, there has been a movement to elevate some styles of rum to recognize spirits that are artisanal and crafted in traditional stills, like single malt Scotch, Cognac, Armagnac, or bourbon. Rum descriptors like "pure single rum" or "single blended rum" are now being used for superpremium rums of today. See "Deciphering rum labels" on pp92–93.

BY COLOUR

Rum classification by colour can be misleading as it implies ageing and certain flavour profiles. However, the colour of a rum has no bearing on its flavour. A gold or dark colour may be influenced by many factors, including how long the rum has spent in the barrel, the age of the barrel (newer barrels add more colour than older ones), or how dark the caramel is. Some white rums are unaged, while others are aged in wood, then filtered to remove the colour. All of these types of rums have dissimilar flavour profiles, so a categorization by colour is merely that.

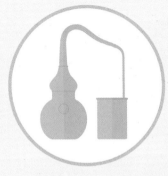
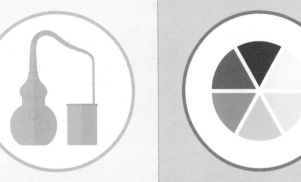

IS SPICED RUM A RUM?

Spiced rum is a flavoured variation of traditional rum and infused with spices, herbs, fruits, or botanicals during the production process. But some purists question whether it's really rum.

ADDED INGREDIENTS

Spiced rum is a versatile spirit, enjoyed both neat and in cocktails, and can offer a flavourful alternative to traditional rums. Added spices, such as cinnamon, vanilla, or nutmeg, fruits, and botanicals impart distinct flavours and aromas, enhancing the rum's complexity and depth.

Despite its popularity and widespread use in mixed drinks, however, spiced rum has faced criticism from purists, who argue that the addition of spices and other ingredients masks the true character of the rum itself. Indeed, some spiced rums can be overly sweet or artificially flavoured, lacking the depth and complexity of unadulterated rum. There are,

however, many artisanal spiced rums on the market that use high-quality ingredients and traditional infusion methods to create a balanced and nuanced spirit.

WHAT IS SPICED RUM?

One of the key elements in the definition of spiced rum is the absence of strict regulations governing its production. Unlike some other spirits, there is no universally agreed-upon standard for what constitutes spiced rum, except that its base should legally be called rum prior to flavouring.

This lack of regulation allows for a wide range of interpretations and variations, contributing to the diversity within the category. In Europe, for instance, a spiced rum needs only to be bottled at 37.5% ABV (the legal minimum for a rum in the EU) to be able to use the word "rum" on its label. However, the label must say "spiced rum" or "flavoured rum".

Note that if the label says "spirit drink", then the product is neither rum nor spiced rum, but rum is "possibly" one of the ingredients within the blend (see "Deciphering rum labels" on pp92–93).

SPICE DROP
Spice Drop is a British spiced rum bottled at 40% ABV

CHAIRMAN'S RESERVE
Chairman's Reserve is a spiced rum made in St Lucia

CAPTAIN MORGAN
Bottled at 35% ABV, Captain Morgan's Spiced Gold is labelled as a spirit drink

SPICED RUMS
Legally, spiced rums are not rums, but are simply rums that have been flavoured or altered. In big rum regions such as Europe, North America, and the Caribbean, it is not permitted to flavour a rum and sell it as pure rum, but rum can be used as an ingredient or base, and the product can be sold as a separate class of spirit.

HOW SPICED RUMS ARE MADE

There are several methods for spicing rum, each contributing to the unique flavour profile of the final product.

MACERATION
One common approach is maceration, where spices and botanicals are steeped directly in the rum base. This method allows for a more direct infusion of flavours and is often used for small-batch productions or artisanal spiced rums.

SPICE BLENDS
Another method involves the use of spice blends or extracts, where pre-prepared mixtures of spices are added to the rum. This approach offers consistency in flavour and allows for precise control over the final product's taste profile.

AGEING RUM IN BARRELS
Some distilleries may also age rum in barrels that previously housed spices to impart additional flavour complexity to the spiced rum.

BOTANICAL RUMS: THE NEW GIN?

Recently, some distillers have started distilling their spiced rums with botanicals or spices added directly to the still, similar to how gin is made. The resulting spicy spirit can also be blended with unspiced rums. This method can result in a more subtle and integrated flavour profile, with the spices becoming fully incorporated into the spirit during distillation.

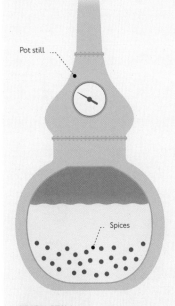

Pot still

Spices

SPICY STILL
Distillers add spices or botanicals directly to the still. Some new European brands use a botanicals chamber on the still.

A LITTLE TOT OF
------- RUM'S -------
HISTORY

THE HISTORY OF RUM is a fascinating journey that begins with the cultivation of sugarcane in ancient times. As it journeyed from east to west, technological advancement helped to liberate the spirit of the cane through fermentation and distillation. Thanks to trade and exploration, sugarcane reached the Americas and flourished, in part due to the tropical climate and also enabled by the enslaved labour and servitude in the region. Sugarcane was eventually transformed into rum, resulting in a diverse product that reflected the regional, cultural, and ancestral influences of the rum makers. Rum's popularity among sailors, traders, and explorers led to it spreading from the Caribbean to Europe, becoming a global commodity that, in some way or another, has shaped the world.

THE SPREAD OF SUGARCANE

In the lush landscapes of the globe's tropical regions, where sunlight kisses the earth and fertile soil yields abundant harvests, people have long harnessed the sweet nectar of sugarcane to craft a symphony of beverages.

IT STARTS WITH SUGARCANE

Before the heady days when Rumbullion (also known as kill devil, see pp28–31) was drunk in the Caribbean basin, the rest of the world was already awash with an array of sugarcane-based libations (see pp14–17). These drinks arose from ancient traditions and local ingenuity, whispered stories of cultures intertwined with nature's sweet bounty. From the aromatic Batavia arrack of Indonesia to the refreshing *guarapo* of the Andes and the vibrant *cachaça* of Brazil, the prelude to rum is a tale of innovation, resourcefulness, and the artistry of fermentation. These culturally created drinks paved the way for the rum revolution, offering a tantalizing glimpse into the tastes and customs of bygone eras.

The exact date of the discovery of sugarcane is not well documented, as it occurred in ancient times before written

LAKATOI OUTRIGGER
This illustration from the 1880s depicts a *lakatoi*, a vessel used for trading around New Guinea.

POLYNESIANS CARRIED SUGARCANE BY SEA ON THEIR MIGRATIONS, CHEWING THE STALKS TO BOOST ENERGY.

records were widely kept. However, sugarcane is believed to have originated in the Polynesian islands around New Guinea about 8000 BCE, with its cultivation dating back thousands of years.

One of the reasons experts believe this is because of the relationship between an indigenous beetle species and the New Guinean fly. The beetle feeds on sugarcane, without which it cannot survive, and the fly parasitizes the beetle, without which it, too, cannot live. For this relationship to have evolved, experts believe sugarcane must have been established in this region for thousands of years.

SUGARCANE MIGRATIONS

Over the following years, Polynesians carried sugarcane with them on their sea migrations, chewing the stalks to boost energy. They took it to Indonesia, the Philippines, and the northern part of India about 1000 BCE. Later, it travelled to Fiji, Tonga, Samoa, the Cook Islands, the Marquesas, Easter Island, and Hawaii.

Sugarcane's use as a source of sweetness can also be traced back to ancient civilizations in India,

CACHAÇA: RUM'S COUSIN

Portuguese Pedro Álvares Cabral was the first European to land in Brazil, in 1500. At the time, two new crazes were sweeping across Europe: sugar made from sugarcane, and alcohol distilled in Arabic pot stills, such as genever (a gin-like spirit) and brandy. As well as planting sugarcane, the Portuguese brought these new technologies to Brazil, and set up three sugar mills in 1532, 1533, and 1543. They installed copper alembic stills (see p68) to turn sugarcane wine into *aguardiente de caña*, which would eventually be known as *cachaça*. This was 100 years before the British started "rumming" in the Caribbean (see pp36–37).

BRAZILIAN BEVERAGE
Distilled from sugarcane juice, *cachaça* is one of the most popular alcoholic drinks in Brazil.

where sugarcane was cultivated and used for its sweet juice.

Tenth-century Arab geographer and scholar al-Masudi included one of the first detailed descriptions of a sugar mill in his book *Muruj ad-Dhahab wa-Ma'adin al-Jawhar* (*Meadows of Gold and Mines of Gems*). His description provides an

early glimpse into methods used for sugar production in ancient India. This involved extracting juice from sugarcane through crushing and pressing, followed by boiling it to produce sugar and molasses. These mills were likely a precursor to more advanced sugar mills that emerged in later centuries.

"A REED IN INDIA BRINGS FORTH HONEY WITHOUT THE HELP OF BEES, FROM WHICH AN INTOXICATING DRINK IS MADE THOUGH THE PLANT BEARS NO FRUIT."

INDIAN SUGARCANE WINE

It is said that in 325 BCE, Nearchus, a general in Alexander the Great's army, wrote that he had found "a reed in India [that] brings forth honey without the help of bees, from which an intoxicating drink is made though the plant bears no fruit". Sanskrit words for fermented sugarcane drinks already existed – *sīdhu* and *gaud* – suggesting that Nearchus may have drunk this sugarcane wine in India. Although these drinks were not rum, as they were not distilled, here was an intoxicating drink from a magical plant that could be cultivated easily to give a product similar to honey but in greater quantities – and with less risk of bee stings.

THE FIRST DISTILLERS

Centuries later, the Egyptians were arguably the first distillers. When the Arab Saracens overran Egypt in the 7th century CE, they brought with them the new honey substitute. The Egyptians may have experimented with this, but if they did, there are no records of the name of the sugarcane spirit.

NEARCHUS
Nearchus undertook a voyage from the Indus River to the mouth of the Tigris River following Alexander the Great's Indian campaign in 326–324 BCE. He recorded that sugarcane was one of the commodities that were cultivated and traded in the Indus Valley.

THE GLOBAL SPREAD OF SUGAR

This map shows where and when sugarcane spread around the world from its origin in the Polynesian islands around New Guinea in 8000 BCE.

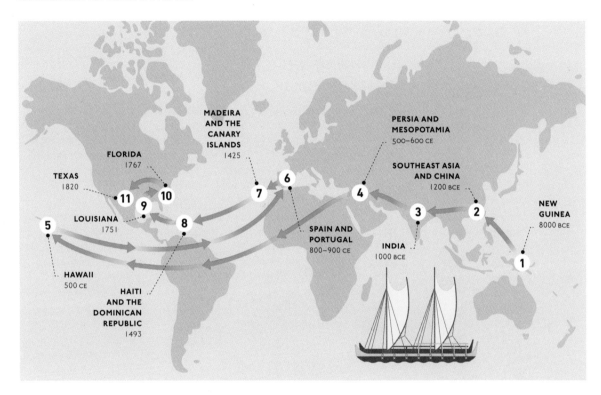

MADEIRA AND THE CANARY ISLANDS
1425

PERSIA AND MESOPOTAMIA
500–600 CE

SOUTHEAST ASIA AND CHINA
1200 BCE

FLORIDA
1767

TEXAS
1820

NEW GUINEA
8000 BCE

LOUISIANA
1751

INDIA
1000 BCE

SPAIN AND PORTUGAL
800–900 CE

HAWAII
500 CE

HAITI AND THE DOMINICAN REPUBLIC
1493

SUGARCANE SPREADS AROUND THE WORLD

The Saracens passed the science of sugarcane cultivation and growing to the Arab Moors, who, in turn, took it, along with cane cuttings, across the Mediterranean to Granada in the Iberian peninsula, which they conquered and occupied from 711 to 1492 CE. By 1150, the Moors had cultivated approximately 30,350 hectares (75,000 acres) of sugarcane.

They also planted cane in the Canary Islands off the west coast of Africa.

SUGARCANE IN THE NEW WORLD

In 1493, Christopher Columbus set sail again, after previously landing in the Bahamas, Cuba, and Hispaniola (Dominican Republic and Haiti). This time, he took with him several sugarcane experts from Africa and hundreds of sugarcane shoots, with the intention of growing the shoots in the New World. The sugarcane, originally gathered from the Canary Islands, was first planted in Hispaniola that same year. Over the next 30 years, the Spanish planted cane in Puerto Rico, Jamaica, Cuba, and Mexico. The Portuguese – not to be outdone by the Spanish – also ventured across the Atlantic, seeking their fortune and planting valuable sugarcane, but they focused on South America, especially Brazil.

KILL DEVIL TO RUMBULLION

In the 17th and 18th centuries, Barbados emerged as a cradle for the birth of rum, laying the foundation for what would become one of the Caribbean's most iconic and cherished spirits.

SUGARCANE ON BARBADOS

This period marked the convergence of European colonization, the flourishing sugarcane industry, the ingenuity of Barbadian settlers, and the spirit-making knowledge of enslaved Africans, resulting in the creation of a spirit that would shape the island's identity for centuries to come.

Europeans from South America brought their knowledge of sugarcane cultivation to the coral island of Barbados. With its fertile soil and tropical climate, it was an ideal location for sugarcane to flourish. British settlers, who first colonized the island in 1625, were drawn by the promise of wealth and opportunity and began establishing sugarcane plantations across the island. As sugarcane production expanded, so did the need for cheap labour, leading to the importation of enslaved people to work the lands.

Sugarcane quickly became the cornerstone of Barbados's local economy, fuelling a thriving agricultural industry that would come to dominate the island's landscape. However, the process

BARBADOS
A painting by the Dutch artist Isaac Sailmaker depicts the island of Barbados in about 1694.

MAPPING BARBADOS
A map of Barbados from
1752 shows not only the
towns, churches, roads, and
fortifications on the island,
but also plantations and
sugar works.

of refining sugarcane into sugar was a labour-intensive and time-consuming endeavour, and plantation owners were constantly searching for ways to maximize their yield and profitability.

It was amid this backdrop of industry, innovation, and know-how that rum(bullion), as it was known, was born or, at least, its alias, kill devil.

THE ORIGIN OF RUM

Plantation owners soon realized that fermenting and distilling sugarcane juice and molasses produced a potent and flavourful drink that could not only be consumed but also used as currency to trade goods and services. Rum was a valuable source of income for the Barbadian planters and, sadly, became a part of everyday life for enslaved Africans and indentured plantation workers.

The exact date and origins of rum in Barbados are shrouded in myth, but it is widely believed that the spirit was first distilled on the island sometime in the early to mid-17th century. French scholar Alain Huetz de Lemps believes that rum was being made on the island by at least 1638, if not before. One of the earliest documents to use the term "rum" is a plantation deed recorded in Barbados in 1650.

Early Barbadian cane spirit was rough and unrefined, earning the nickname "kill devil" for its fiery taste and potent kick. In 1651, the first written reference associating rumbullion with kill devil appeared. English merchant Giles Sylvester wrote: "The chief fuddling they make in Island is Rumbullion alias Kill-Devil, and this is made of sugar canes distilled, a hot, hellish and terrible liquor."

RUMBULLION

The term "rumbullion" was used in England, particularly in Devon, as slang for a tumultuous uproar or commotion. It's believed that this term might have been applied to the fiery and spirited nature of the newly distilled spirit or the consumers that drunk it excessively. Rumbullion eventually evolved into the word "rum", and plantation owners in both French and Spanish colonies eventually adopted the name for their sugarcane spirits, translating it to *rhum* and *ron*, respectively.

BY THE 18TH CENTURY, RUM PRODUCTION IN BARBADOS WAS IN FULL SWING, WITH DOZENS OF DISTILLERIES SCATTERED ACROSS THE ISLAND.

MOUNT GAY RUM
Mount Gay Estate in Barbados was founded in 1703. Before 1801, it was called Mount Gilboa.

THE 18TH CENTURY

As the art of distillation evolved and techniques like double distillation were refined, Barbadian rum began to gain a reputation for its quality and craftsmanship. By the 18th century, rum production in Barbados was in full swing, with dozens of distilleries scattered across the island. These distilleries ranged from small, family-owned operations to large-scale commercial enterprises, each producing rums of varying styles and flavours. Barbadian rum quickly became a prized commodity, sought after by merchants, traders, and sailors around the Americas.

One of the most significant developments in the history of Barbadian rum came in 1703, with the establishment of the Mount Gilboa Estate, in the parish of St Lucy. In 1801, after the death of its estate manager, Sir John Gay Alleyne, the site and distillery were renamed Mount Gay (Mount Alleyne, his family name, had already been taken). Today, Mount Gay is still making rum on the same site, making it the oldest continuous rum-making distillery in the world.

THE GOLDEN ERA

The golden era of rum can be considered to span from the late 17th century to the mid-19th century, a period characterized by the rapid expansion, innovation, and flourishing trade of rum across the Caribbean and beyond.

During this time, rum production underwent significant advancements, particularly in regions like Barbados, Jamaica, and Martinique. The Caribbean islands were ideally suited for cultivating sugarcane, the primary ingredient for rum production, and the booming sugar industry provided ample raw material for distillation.

However, this golden era of rum had its dark side. One of the key factors contributing to this boom period was the rise of the transatlantic slave trade and the exploitation of enslaved labour on sugar plantations.

A triangular trade route (see above right) connected Europe, Africa, and the Americas, with rum playing a role as a commodity

TRIANGLE OF TRADE

European goods including rum were exported to Africa and traded for enlaved Africans, who were sent to work on plantations in the Americas. In exchange for the labour, products such as sugar, tobacco, cotton, and rum were shipped back to Europe from the Americas.

KEY

 RAW MATERIALS (SUGAR, COTTON, TOBACCO) AND RUM

 MANUFACTURED GOODS (FIREARMS, TEXTILES) AND RUM

 ENSLAVED AFRICANS

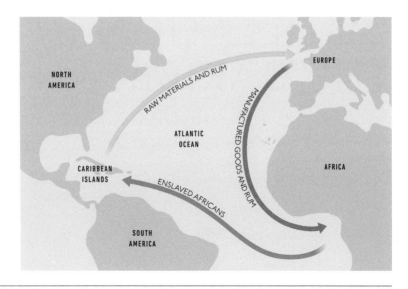

exchanged for enslaved people in West Africa and goods in Europe. The trade network facilitated the widespread distribution of rum to markets around the world, and helped to build the foundation for colonial superpowers such as Britain, France, and Spain. But the profitability of sugar and rum production came at the expense of human suffering and abuse.

RUM BEDS IN

The 18th century in particular saw the establishment of numerous rum distilleries across the Caribbean, each developing its unique techniques and styles. Barbados, often regarded as the birthplace of rum, was renowned for its high-quality, smooth rums, while Jamaica became famous for

its full-bodied, flavourful varieties. Rum became ingrained in the social and economic fabric of the Caribbean islands, and continued being a form of currency and a trade commodity. For those who were trafficked or born into servitude, it became an integral part of cultural celebrations, rituals, and a connection to the spirit world of their ancestors.

LOADING RUM
A 19th-century print by British artist William Clark shows enslaved labourers loading barrels of rum onto ships in Antigua.

DISTILLATION IN THE CARIBBEAN

The history of distillation in the Caribbean islands is a melting pot of stories that combines the evolution of both batch and continuous distillation methods, reflecting the region's rich cultural and economic history.

THE ANCIENT INFLUENCE

Early distillation in the Caribbean was conducted entirely in traditional pot, or alembic, stills (see p68), which were simple in design and rooted in traditional alembic technology from ancient times. Distillation involved heating fermented sugarcane juice, skimmings or scum (the frothy layer of impurities that rise to the surface during the fermentation of molasses), and molasses in a pot still or kettle, usually made of metal. This allowed the alcohol vapours to rise, and they were then condensed back into a liquid.

This method of batch distillation was further innovated when Barbados rum makers began double distilling their rums to make them flavoursome and much sought after in the region.

THE DOUBLE RETORT STILL

While the earliest distillation methods in the Caribbean had their benefits, they also posed limitations, particularly in achieving higher alcohol by volume (ABV) levels. With a single batch distillation, the maximum ABV attainable from a wash (fermented sugarcane juice or molasses) of 8–10% ABV was

RUM DISTILLERY
Enslaved people labouring at a rum distillery in Antigua are depicted in this 1823 print by British artist William Clark.

DOUBLE RETORT STILLS BECAME ICONIC SYMBOLS OF BRITISH WEST INDIAN RUM PRODUCTION.

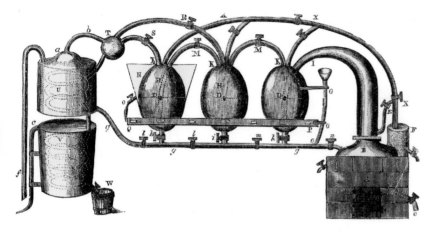

THE ADAM STILL
This wood engraving shows the still designed by Édouard Adam, patented in 1801. The double retort still was misnamed the Adams still by Eurocentric historians.

around 45%. However, to achieve a higher proof, the spirit had to be redistilled, which was costly and inefficient, requiring the still to be emptied and refilled for each run.

In a stroke of ingenuity, a distiller conceived the idea of connecting the pot still to two smaller pots, known as retorts. One retort contained low wine (the first distillate) at 35% ABV, while the other held high wine (the second distillate) at 55–70% ABV. This configuration enabled the spirit to undergo three distillations in a single pass, resulting in a product with an ABV of 85% or more.

This double retort still, misnamed the Adam still (after the still invented by Frenchman Édouard Adam), was introduced to Jamaica during the early 19th century, and marked a pivotal moment in the island's rum-making history. Double retort stills, often made of copper, became iconic symbols of British West Indian rum production, especially in Jamaica, as distillers embraced the artistry of batch distillation, creating traditional rums with distinctive profiles.

CONTINUOUS DISTILLATION

With the Industrial Revolution sweeping much of the world by the late 18th century, the region witnessed a leap forward in spirit production with the introduction of continuous distillation methods, notably the Coffey, or patent, still (see p70). Irish inventor and distiller Aeneas Coffey's improvement of the continuous still in the 1830s revolutionized spirit production globally, offering increased efficiency and production scalability.

Continuous distillation involves a continuous flow of wash through a series of columns, allowing for the separation of alcohol from other components. Distillation could now be done without having to stop and start as with the old pot stills. Columns were also advantageous for producing lighter rums, and catered to the growing demand for consistent and versatile spirits.

In the early 20th century, some Caribbean distilleries began adopting continuous stills, initially in conjunction with traditional pot stills, and then eventually replacing batch distillation, especially in countries such as Cuba and Martinique. But rum powers such as Barbados and Jamaica stood firm with pot stills, as their popular style of rum depended on being made in the old, traditional way.

POT STILL
The River Antoine Distillery in Grenada, established in 1785, uses a traditional double retort pot still to make its rum.

THE MODERN ERA

As the Caribbean entered the modern era, many distilleries found a balance between batch and continuous distillation methods. Some retained the artistry of pot stills for crafting high-ester rums with bold and complex flavours, while integrating continuous distillation for producing lighter and more neutral rums.

The modern era also brought economic shifts, including changes in global demand and fluctuations in the price of sugar, which impacted the profitability of individual distilleries. Smaller distilleries often struggled to compete with larger, more efficient operations and were closed down or sold.

As larger distilleries acquired smaller ones or merged with competitors, the industry became more centralized. This consolidation allowed companies to streamline operations, reduce costs, and increase efficiency. The introduction of more advanced distillation technologies, such as multi-column stills (see p71), allowed for greater production capacity and cost-effectiveness. Smaller, traditional pot stills became less common as distilleries modernized their equipment for distilling.

THE MODERN ERA BROUGHT ECONOMIC SHIFTS THAT IMPACTED THE PROFITABILITY OF INDIVIDUAL DISTILLERIES.

RUM SHACK
A rum shop or rum shack in the Caribbean is the centre of the local community – a place to meet and talk about current affairs, as well drink, eat, and often buy groceries.

THE CRAFT RUM REVIVAL

In recent decades, the craft rum movement has seen a resurgence of interest in traditional pot stills and artisanal distillation methods. Particularly in Barbados, Jamaica, and Guyana, distilleries proudly highlight their commitment to traditional batch distillation, emphasizing *terroir*, and producing rums that capture the essence of the local sugarcane and regional molasses.

The Caribbean's history of rum distillation is a dynamic tale of adaptation and innovation, where the marriage of batch and continuous distillation methods has contributed to the region's reputation as a diverse and influential force in the world of rum. The coexistence of traditional pot stills and modern column stills, sometimes in the same distillery, showcases the resilience and creativity of Caribbean distillers, preserving heritage while embracing progress in the pursuit of crafting exceptional rums.

RUM MOBILE
A pickup advertises Tortuga rum in Grand Cayman. The company was founded in 1984.

THE BRITISH INFLUENCE: JAMAICA

The introduction of rum production to Jamaica is attributed to the British, who captured the island from the Spanish in 1655. Rum production became an integral part of the island's economy.

RUM IN JAMAICA TIMELINE

1494–1655

The Spanish cultivate sugarcane and other crops on the island after Christopher Columbus colonizes it in 1494, but there is limited evidence to suggest that they distil sugarcane juice or molasses in Jamaica before the British arrive in 1655. The Spanish primarily use Jamaica as a strategic base for their expeditions and focus on extracting gold rather than establishing large-scale agricultural operations.

18TH CENTURY

Jamaica emerges as a major player in the rum trade, exporting large quantities to Europe. The island's fertile soil helps sugarcane cultivation to expand rapidly, and rum production becomes a vital part of the island's economy. Colonizers profiteer from the knowledge contributed by enslaved Africans of fermentation and distillation techniques, laying the foundation for the Jamaican rum-making tradition. European plantation owners become wealthy selling rum and sugar.

19TH CENTURY

Jamaica experiences a boom in rum production, fuelled by growing global demand for alcohol. Distillers seek to enhance efficiency, leading to innovations such as the use of double retort pot stills (see p33). At the Centennial International Exhibition in Philadelphia in 1876, Jamaican rum wins gold medals and gains international recognition for its bold flavours and aromatic profile, which become synonymous with its style.

WHITNEY ESTATE
An engraving by James Hakewill shows the sugar plantation at Whitney Estate in Jamaica in the early 19th century.

STAMP OF APPROVAL
A Jamaican postage stamp from 1939 celebrates the domestic sugar industry.

EARLY 20TH CENTURY

Jamaican rum continues to thrive, despite the challenges of World War I (1914–18) and Prohibition in the United States (1920–33), which have a negative impact on Jamaican rum exports. However, the rise of the tiki cocktail culture after Prohibition helps popularize rum cocktails, further boosting the spirit's global appeal. Companies like J. Wray & Nephew play a pivotal role in shaping Jamaica's reputation as a premium rum producer.

LATE 20TH CENTURY

Jamaica witnesses a resurgence of interest in traditional, artisanal rum. Distilleries embrace small-batch production methods and emphasize quality over quantity. The island's rum industry benefits from tourism, with visitors eager to experience the rich history and flavours of Jamaican rum. Sustainable practices and social responsibility become priorities for many distilleries.

21ST CENTURY

Today, the island's six remaining distilleries explore new techniques and flavour profiles while staying true to their heritage. In 2016, all Jamaican producers agree to a geographical indication (GI; see p13) for Jamaica rum. This means that all products that have the term "Jamaica Rum" on the label must adhere to the rules stated in the GI when sold in a country where the GI is registered.

JAMAICA'S RUM INDUSTRY BENEFITS FROM TOURISM, WITH VISITORS EAGER TO EXPERIENCE THE RICH HISTORY AND FLAVOURS OF JAMAICAN RUM.

TRAVEL POSTER
Tourism in Jamaica took off in the 20th century. This poster from the 1920s promotes the country as an attractive tropical destination.

THE FRENCH INFLUENCE: MARTINIQUE

Martinique is seen as one of the cradles of the rum industry. French colonizers, exploiting the labour and expertise of enslaved people, started making sugar at a similar time as their British neighbours in Barbados.

RUM IN MARTINIQUE TIMELINE

17TH CENTURY

The French arrive in 1635 to colonize the island. In 1644, Benjamin Da Costa, a Dutchman from Brazil, introduces sugar-making equipment and brings one of the first alembic stills to Martinique. By the 1650s, French rum makers are making *eau de vie de canne* (sugarcane brandy) by distilling the scum from sugar-making products.

18TH CENTURY

In 1713, by royal decree, King Louis XIV prohibits the sale of Caribbean rum in France to protect the interests of domestic distillers and maintain control over the spirits market. This prompts distillers to explore alternative markets for their products, like Canada. The importation ban lasts until 1777. Britain captures Martinique in 1762 and brings its rum-making knowledge, improving the quality of Martinican rums. In 1763, Martinique is again under French rule.

EARLY 19TH CENTURY

During the Napoleonic Wars (1803–15) with France, Britain prevents the French West Indies from trading with America and British colonies, and export sales suffer. Larger distilleries eventually put the smaller ones out of business. The larger distilleries use local molasses to create rum on an industrial scale, called *rhum industriel*, while the small plantation distilleries craft their rums from sugarcane juice, calling their product *rhum agricole* (agricultural rum).

RHUM AGRICOLE
Martinique is renowned for its production of high-quality *rhum agricole*, which benefits from the island's volcanic soil and tropical climate.

SMALL PLANTATION DISTILLERIES CRAFT THEIR RUMS FROM SUGARCANE JUICE, CALLING THEIR PRODUCT *RHUM AGRICOLE*.

MARTINIQUE AOC RUM
Rums that have the words *"appellation d'origine contrôllée"* (AOC) on the label certify the rums' authenticity, quality, and adherence to traditional production methods.

MID- TO LATE 19TH CENTURY

France's grape vines are devastated, first by a powdery mildew called oidium in the 1850s, and then in the 1870s by phylloxera, an insect pest. These catastrophes result in suspensions of import duty on rum from the Caribbean to replenish alcohol supplies in France. This is great news for French West Indian rum makers. By the late 19th century, millions of litres of *rhum* are imported into France, with Martinique being the leading supplier.

20TH CENTURY

In 1902, the Mount Pelée volcano erupts, killing more than 30,000 people and destroying the city of Saint-Pierre, the centre of the Martinican *rhum* industry, which disrupts production and supply chains. In 1923, the French government implements quotas on how much *rhum* can be imported from Martinique and the French Caribbean. Over the next 25 years, many of the 150 *rhum* distilleries on Martinique close due to the quota system.

LATE 20TH CENTURY

In 1996, the *appellation d'origine contrôlée* (AOC) for Martinique *rhum agricole* is officially established, setting strict criteria for the production of this unique spirit. The AOC ensures that Martinican *rhum agricole* meets specific standards related to geographical origin, raw materials, fermentation, distillation, and ageing.

MOUNT PELÉE
The eruption of Mount Pelée in 1902 devastated the city of Saint-Pierre, which was never fully restored to its former glory.

THE SPANISH INFLUENCE: CUBA

Sugarcane was brought to Cuba in 1493 but did not flourish until 1512, when the Spanish returned with 300 men and fresh sugarcane seedlings. By 1570, there were sugar plantations and mills throughout the country.

RUM IN CUBA TIMELINE

17TH CENTURY

By 1620, there are at least 50 sugar mills in Cuba, with mentions of *aguardiente de caña* dating back to 1643. A local spirit made from molasses, *chiringuito*, is produced in small amounts. In 1693, the Spanish Crown prohibits rum- and alcohol-making in all the Spanish colonies as they threaten the Spanish brandy and wine industries.

EARLY 18TH CENTURY

In 1714, a new royal decree prohibits the production and sale "of the beverage *aguardiente de caña* in the Kingdoms of the Indies". Since previous bans have not had the desired effect, this time not only is production prohibited, but also all pot stills and other equipment used to produce the spirit are to be destroyed. Owners are fined 10 pesos.

LATE 18TH CENTURY

In 1762, the British capture the capital, Havana, for 11 months, bringing new cane-growing and refining techniques, and importing more than 4,000 enslaved Africans to work on plantations and make rum. In 1782, the American colonies' rum supply from the British colonies is cut off, resulting in more Cuban rum being sold into North America.

EARLY 19TH CENTURY

To expand the market for rum, the Spanish Royal Development Board offers a prize for improving the rum-making process. Cuba embraces the Industrial Revolution as it sweeps the world. In 1827, there are about 300 distilleries in Cuba. Enabled by enslaved labourers, the first railway is built in 1837, easing the transportation of sugarcane and molasses.

CUBAN RAILWAY
A postcard from about 1910 depicts sugarcane being transported by train to a refinery.

BACARDÍ POSTER
A poster from the 1920s promotes BACARDÍ rum as an ingredient in the recipe for the Cuba Libre cocktail.

LATE 19TH CENTURY

Many Cuban rums, which are lighter than other Caribbean rums, start to appear on the local market. In 1876, at the International Centennial Exposition, in Philadelphia, Bacardí wins an award, beating Jamaican rums, considered the best at the time. In 1898, the Spanish-American war in Cuba introduces many American soldiers to rum.

EARLY 20TH CENTURY

Cuba is one of the first Caribbean countries to introduce column stills. Bacardí retires its pot still in 1911, cementing the Cuban style of light rum. Prohibition in the United States (1920–33) results in thousands of thirsty Americans making the short trip to Cuba, where they can legally drink. Bacardí sets up distilleries in Mexico (1931) and Puerto Rico (1936).

LATE 20TH CENTURY

In 1959, the Cuban Revolution (1953–59) leads to the nationalization of many rum distilleries. Assets are seized and many rum companies either cease production or relocate to other countries. This has a crippling effect on rum exports, made worse when the US sets an embargo on all trade with Cuba in 1962, banning the importation of Cuban rums into America.

21ST CENTURY

In 2023, the Cuban government applies to register Cuba as a geographical indication (GI; see p13) for rum in the European Union (EU) geographical indications register. If passed, then only rums made in Cuba according to local rules and regulations can display the *sello de garantía* (seal of guarantee) if sold in the EU.

CUBA IS ONE OF THE FIRST CARIBBEAN COUNTRIES TO EXPERIMENT WITH COLUMN STILLS.

LIQUOR BELT
An American tourist in Havana shows off her ingenious belt for smuggling liquor into the United States in 1932 during Prohibition.

NAVY RUM RATIONS

Rum rations in the British Royal Navy have a history that spans centuries, shaping naval culture and traditions while playing a crucial role in maintaining the morale and wellbeing of sailors at sea. From its inception in the 17th century to its eventual abolition in the 20th century, rum rations left an indelible mark on maritime history.

THE DAILY TOT

In the mid-17th century, sailors were provided with a daily allotment of beer, but concerns about spoilage and limited storage capacity led to the introduction of rum as a more practical alternative. It was cheaper, easier to store, and, because of its higher alcohol by volume (ABV), less prone to spoilage than beer, making it an ideal choice for long sea voyages.

The rations served multiple purposes aboard navy ships. Beyond its practical advantages, rum was erroneously believed to have medicinal properties that could ward off scurvy, a common affliction caused by vitamin C deficiency. Additionally, rum helped alleviate the monotony and hardships of life at sea, providing sailors with a brief respite from the rigours of service.

The daily rum ration, or "tot", was typically distributed to sailors in the late morning and early afternoon. The tot size varied over time and depended on factors such as rank, duration of the voyage, and prevailing regulations.

THE DAILY TOT
A cigarette card published by Player's Cigarettes in 1905 shows sailors receiving their daily tot.

In the 18th and 19th centuries, the standard tot size was around half a pint (about 285ml) of rum per sailor per day.

GROG ON BOARD

In 1740, the admiral of the fleet, Edward Vernon, introduced the practice of diluting sailors' rum rations with water and lime juice to prevent excessive drunkenness. The admiral's nickname was Old Grog because of the waterproof grogram (grosgrain) cloak he wore, and the diluted rum ration became known as "grog".

The distribution of rum rations was accompanied by rituals and traditions that became ingrained in naval culture. Sailors formed orderly queues to receive their tots, often accompanied by the call of "splice the mainbrace".

NAVY RUM
A magazine advertisement from the 1920s promotes Wood's 100 Old Navy Rum, a brand that is still made today.

BLACK TOT DAY

Despite its popularity among sailors, rum rations in the Royal Navy came under scrutiny in the 20th century due to concerns about alcohol consumption and its impact on discipline and efficiency. On 31 July 1970, following recommendations from the Admiralty Board, the Royal Navy officially abolished the daily issue of rum rations. This day was dubbed "Black Tot Day".

The legacy of rum rations lives on in naval folklore, popular culture, and rum brands. Pusser's Rum, for instance, takes its name from the purser, who issued the rum ration on ships. The brand Black Tot incorporates some of the original pre-1970s rums in its blend. Today, although there is no formal definition of navy strength rum, it is essentially a commercial spirit bottled at between 54.5% and 57% ABV.

THE STANDARD TOT SIZE WAS AROUND HALF A PINT OF RUM PER SAILOR PER DAY.

A TIMELINE OF NAVY RUM

While daily rum rations may be a thing of the past, the legacy of this tradition lives on in the collective memory of the Royal Navy and continues to be commemorated today.

TIMELINE OF NAVY RUM

17TH CENTURY

In 1655, Admiral William Penn issues sugarcane spirit to the sailors in his fleet. Navy regulations stipulate that, in the absence of beer rations, wine, brandy, or rum will suffice to be given to sailors in half-pint (285ml) measures.

EARLY 18TH CENTURY

In 1731, the Navy Board makes official the daily ration of 1 pint (570ml) of wine or half a pint (two gills/285ml) of rum, to be issued neat in two equal amounts daily. In 1740, Admiral Edward Vernon orders the dilution of sailors' rum with water to stretch the supply and prevent excessive drunkenness. This diluted mixture, known as "grog", eventually replaces beer as the standard daily ration. Lime and sugar are added to the blend for palatability. This practice likely leads to the Americans calling the British "limeys". Later, it is realized that the citrus also prevents scurvy.

LATE 18TH CENTURY

In 1798, James Man of ED & F Man, a London brokerage firm, secures the sole contract to supply the Royal Navy with rum for the daily "rum tot". The firm acquires rum in bulk from Trinidad, Barbados, Demerara, and Jamaica to be shipped to London and blended.

ADMIRAL WILLIAM PENN
Sir William Penn (1621–70) was a noted English admiral and member of parliament.

JAMES LIND
In 1747, Scottish naval surgeon James Lind experimented with different cures for scurvy on board navy ships. Later, he concluded that citrus fruits were the most effective remedy. Today, we know that scurvy is caused by a deficiency in vitamin C, found in citrus fruits.

WORLD WAR II
The flight deck crew of a Royal Navy aircraft carrier are issued with their daily tot of rum in 1945 during World War II.

19TH CENTURY

Rations are cut in half to a quarter of a pint (140ml) a day in 1823. In 1850, the abolition of the rum ration is debated in Parliament and revisited in 1881, but no action is taken on either occasion. During the 1850s, the Royal Navy establishes formal regulations governing the distribution of rum rations. The amount of rum issued to sailors varies based on rank, with stricter controls implemented to prevent excessive consumption and maintain discipline on board ships. The ration is cut to one-eighth of a pint (70ml) for ordinary seamen.

20TH CENTURY

During the two World Wars (1914–18) and (1939–45), rum rations play a significant role in boosting morale among sailors serving in the Royal Navy. The daily tot provides a moment of respite and camaraderie amid the challenges of wartime service. In 1970, changing attitudes towards alcohol consumption and concerns about its impact on discipline and efficiency lead to the decision to discontinue the centuries-old tradition. On 31 July, the Admiralty Board announces the cessation of daily rum rations for Royal Navy sailors. This is later dubbed "Black Tot Day".

21ST CENTURY

While daily rum rations are discontinued, the tradition continues to be commemorated in Royal Navy special occasions such as Trafalgar Night, which celebrates the Royal Navy's victory at the Battle of Trafalgar in 1805. These often include a symbolic issuance of rum to sailors, honouring the rich history and significance of rum rations in naval culture.

ON 31 JULY 1970, THE ADMIRALTY BOARD ANNOUNCES THE CESSATION OF DAILY RUM RATIONS FOR ROYAL NAVY SAILORS.

BLACK TOT RUM
Black Tot Master Blender's Reserve is a premium rum that is a tribute to Black Tot Day, when the daily rum ration was discontinued.

RUM IN OTHER CARIBBEAN REGIONS

The history of rum in the Caribbean from the 17th century onwards was dominated by Britain, France, and Spain, but other colonial powers also had roles in rum's history in the Caribbean region.

PORTUGUESE INFLUENCE

The Portuguese were among the earliest European colonizers of the "New World". They established sugar plantations and mills in Brazil and off the coast of Africa in Madeira and São Tomé and Príncipe. Brazilian plantations laid the groundwork for future spirit production, as the excess molasses and cane juice became the key ingredient in the Brazilian version of *aguardiente de caña*, called *cachaça*. During the early 1600s, Dutch migrants and experts in sugar cultivation, sugar-making equipment, and distillation brought spirit-making knowledge to the Caribbean from Brazil, leading to the birth of Barbadian and Martinican rums.

The Portuguese direct influence on Caribbean rum production was

PERNAMBUCO
An illustrated map of Pernambuco in Brazil depicts a sugar plantation. Dutch migrants and experts from Pernambuco brought spirit-making knowledge to the Caribbean.

THE DUTCH FOCUSED ON SUGAR CULTIVATION AND ESTABLISHED SUGAR PLANTATIONS THROUGHOUT THEIR COLONIES.

small, as other colonial powers, particularly Britain and France, gained dominance in the region. Today, mostly all rums with connections to Portugal come from Madeira (see pp154–55), which is one of the many protected geographical indicator (GI; see p13) rum regions in the European Union (EU), along with Martinique, Guadeloupe, and Demerara in Guyana.

DUTCH INFLUENCE

The Dutch established colonies in the Caribbean and South America during the 17th century, primarily in present-day Suriname, Aruba, Curaçao, and other islands in the Dutch Caribbean. Like their Portuguese counterparts, the Dutch focused on sugar cultivation and established sugar plantations throughout their colonies.

Dutch traders played a pivotal role in the transatlantic slave trade, supplying labour for sugar plantations and ensuring a steady supply of raw materials for rum production, including sugarcane from Brazil, to Barbados and Martinique in the early 1630s.

Dutch distillers brought their expertise to the Caribbean, contributing to the development

DUTCH CARIBBEAN
Enslaved Africans are shown labouring at a sugar mill in the Dutch Caribbean in this line engraving from the 17th century.

of rum as a commercial product. The most notable Dutch contribution to Caribbean rum production was the pot still, the key distillation apparatus used to make spirits such as genever (a gin-like spirit) in Europe and *cachaça* in Brazil. Pot stills allowed for greater control over the distillation process, resulting in higher-quality rums, and would eventually dominate the spirits

world until the use of continuous column stills during the latter half of the 19th century.

Today, the Dutch rum market is relatively small compared to those of the former colonies governed by the British, French, and Spanish. Suriname, previously Dutch Guiana, still exports rum to Europe via the Netherlands, with brands like Black Cat and Borgoe (see p165) its biggest representations.

RUM PRODUCTION BECAME ONE OF THE MAIN ECONOMIC DRIVERS OF THE DANISH CARIBBEAN.

DANISH INFLUENCE

The Danish Caribbean, also known as the Danish West Indies, consisted of the islands of St Thomas, St John, and St Croix, with the latter becoming a colony of the Kingdom of Denmark in 1733. The region remained undeveloped until the late 1740s, when investment in the large-scale production of sugarcane began in earnest. The Danish colonists quickly recognized the profitability of rum production, and it became a vital part of the economy alongside sugar growing.

The Danish Caribbean also participated in the triangular trade (see pp30–31), in which rum, along with sugar and molasses, was exported to European cities such as Flensburg, now in north Germany. Rum production became one of the main economic drivers of the Danish Caribbean, particularly on the island of St Croix, where many distilleries were established. Danish planters and merchants amassed wealth from the rum trade, and the industry thrived during the 18th and 19th centuries.

CHRISTIANSTED
Christiansted on Saint Croix was the former capital of the Danish Caribbean. This illustration from the 19th century shows it as a thriving port.

A. H. Riise's Old St. Croix Rum Factory.   Charlotte Amalie, V. I.

RUM FACTORY
A postcard from the mid-20th century depicts
A.H. Riise's rum factory in Charlotte Amalie,
the capital of the US Virgin Islands.

The abolition of slavery in the Danish Caribbean in 1848 led to significant changes in the sugar and rum industries. With the loss of slave labour, sugar and rum production declined. Changes in global trade and competition from other rum-producing regions, such as Cuba and Jamaica, further contributed to the decline of the Danish Caribbean rum industry.

US VIRGIN ISLANDS

In 1917, amid concerns about the security of the Danish Caribbean during World War I (1914–18),
Denmark sold the islands to the United States, which renamed them the United States Virgin Islands. After the transfer to the United States, some rum production continued on the islands, but it never regained its former prominence, especially after Prohibition in the United States (1920–33) decimated the rum industry.

Today, rum is still made on the US Virgin Islands, albeit on a smaller scale compared to historical levels. The islands are known for producing brands such as Cruzan Rum (see p152).

OLD ST CROIX RUM
A 1940s advertisement for Old St Croix rum promotes it as an alternative to whisky in an Old Fashioned.

RUM IN NORTH AMERICA

Until their independence from Britain in 1776, the American colonies' drink of choice was rum. Whether it was imported from the Caribbean or homemade in New England, rum was drunk daily by many of the immigrant settlers of America.

AMERICA'S DRINK

Rum became known as "America's drink" during colonial times due to a combination of factors that deeply intertwined it with the economic, social, and cultural fabric of the American colonies.

In 1664, to support the demand for rum, the first rum distillery in the Thirteen Colonies was set up on Staten Island. A distillery in Boston, Massachusetts, was founded three years later. Rum production emerged as the primary and most lucrative industry in early colonial New England – in part due to its reliance on forced labour. The region evolved into a prominent distilling hub, leveraging its skilled workforce in technical, metalworking, and cooperage trades, as well as its abundant timber resources.

Rum also played a central role in the triangular trade between the Americas, Europe, and Africa (see pp30–31). New England merchants traded goods such as timber, fish, and livestock to the Caribbean in exchange for molasses. This was then distilled into rum in New England distilleries, with a significant portion of the product exported to Africa to trade for enslaved people. This trade network contributed to the economic prosperity of New England and solidified rum's status as a vital commodity in colonial America.

AN AMERICAN INN
Drinkers in an American inn are depicted in this painting by John Lewis Krimmel. Krimmel's works often showed social gatherings, street scenes, and domestic life.

RUM BECAME ASSOCIATED WITH THE PATRIOTIC CAUSE DURING THE WAR OF INDEPENDENCE.

MORNING RUM
In the 18th century, many American colonists started the day with a drink of rum and consumed it with every meal.

Rum also served as a source of revenue for colonial governments through taxes and tariffs.

A PART OF CULTURE

Rum became deeply ingrained in colonial American culture, with taverns serving as social hubs where people gathered to drink, socialize, and conduct business. Rum was consumed by people of all social classes and backgrounds, from wealthy merchants to labourers and sailors. It is estimated that every man, woman, and child in the American colonies consumed an average of 14 litres (3 gallons) of rum per year. It was often mixed with water, molasses, and spices; with fruit juices to create punches; or in cocktails like the Bombo, Flip, or Toddy.

By 1750, there were 63 distilleries in Massachusetts crafting rum, often using molasses sourced from various suppliers in the Caribbean. In some cases, these suppliers included slave traders, who traded molasses to Puritan distillers in exchange for capital. This capital was then used to buy enslaved people from Africa for sale to West Indian sugar planters.

THE AMERICAN WAR OF INDEPENDENCE

Rum played a significant role during the American War of Independence (1775–83), when it was used to boost morale among troops, treat wounds, and facilitate trade and communication. It was also a source of revenue for the Continental Army, with taxes levied on rum sales to fund the war effort.

Rum became associated with the patriotic cause during the war, and many colonists boycotted British goods, including imported rum and molasses, in support of the independence movement.

As the American colonies expanded westward, so too did the production and consumption of rum. Distilleries proliferated in new settlements and frontier towns. Rum became a symbol of colonial identity and resilience, representing the spirit of independence and self-sufficiency among colonists.

RUM BOTTLE
A rum bottle dated 1772, which belonged to Moses Gill, a member of the Sons of Liberty. The group campaigned against British taxation and policies.

THE 19TH CENTURY

By 1802, New England rum distilleries continued to import molasses, this time from Cuba and the French colonies, to make their rums, but the rise of cheaper American whiskey started to rival the local rum trade.

THE 20TH CENTURY

In 1917, Puerto Rico became a US territory, making Puerto Ricans American citizens just in time for Prohibition (1920–33). Later, Puerto Rico would be handsomely rewarded with favourable tax duties on its rums.

Prohibition meant that any rum production in the United States was either driven underground or non-existent. Drinkers fled to Cuba for their liquor, or they bought illegal alcohol from rum runners like William "Bill" McCoy, who was famous for selling unadulterated spirits. The words "Real McCoy" on his crates signalled to consumers that they were getting the genuine article – hence, some say, the term "the real McCoy".

THE RISE OF TIKI CULTURE

In 1934, Donn Beach, the legendary figure in tiki culture and founder of the Don the Beachcomber restaurant chain, opened his first bar in Hollywood, California. It became renowned for its exotic rum cocktails, Polynesian-inspired decor, and immersive atmosphere, laying the

THE LIGHTER STYLE OF RUM BECAME THE DEFAULT RUM STYLE FOR THE AMERICAN PALATE.

foundation for the tiki bar craze that swept across America in the mid-20th century.

The same year, another iconic figure in tiki culture, Victor Bergeron (Trader Vic), opened a restaurant in Oakland, California. Known as Hinky Dink's, it later evolved into Trader Vic's, a chain of Polynesian-themed restaurants famous for its tropical rum cocktails and unique cuisine. Trader Vic's played a significant role in popularizing tiki culture and remains a beloved institution in the world of hospitality and dining.

RUM EXPORTS SKYROCKET

In 1934, Puerto Rico, as a territory of the US, was given favourable import duties. This saw its rum exports to the US jump from 40,000 litres (8,800 gallons) in 1934 to 9 million litres (2 million gallons) in just seven years. By the 1940s, 1.5 million litres (330,000 gallons) of rum were also imported from the US Virgin Islands.

By 1992, Puerto Rico, together with the US Virgin Islands, exported more than 80 million litres (17.6 million gallons) of rum to the United States, dominating the rum market in North America.

The lighter style of rum from Puerto Rico and the US Virgin Islands became the default rum style for the American palate, leaving little room for the big flavours of other Caribbean rums. Coupled with higher duties, rums from Jamaica, Martinique, Barbados, and Guyana will always have an uphill battle to get a market share in the US, one of the world's biggest consumers of rum.

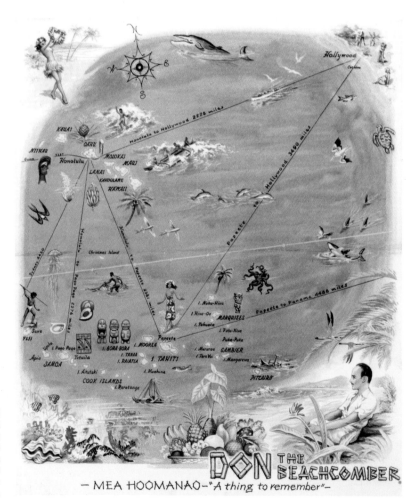

DON THE BEACHCOMBER
A menu card from 1941 for the Don the Beachcomber restaurant chain depicts the iconography of the Polynesian islands.

— MEA HOOMANAO – "A thing to remember" —

RUM IN AUSTRALIA

Rum in Australia is a tale of agricultural innovation, economic endeavours, and a notorious rebellion. The journey begins with sugarcane and evolves through centuries of cultivation, distillation, and the emergence of renowned rum brands.

COLONIAL AUSTRALIA

In 1788, the First Fleet arrived in Australia from Britain, bringing with it not only colonists and convicts, who had been sent to the penal colony by the British government, but also sugarcane. Early attempts at cultivating the crop were not successful, however, and the challenges of adapting it to the unfamiliar Australian climate initially hindered widespread cultivation.

At the time, colonists imported rum from American traders and used it as currency, especially to buy the agricultural services of convicts. Thus as demand increased, the value of rum rose. As a result of widespread drunkenness among the population, governors passed regulations against the illegal sale and distilling of rum. Illegal rum shops, called grog shanties, were destroyed, and any rum found in them was given to local constables.

THE RUM REBELLION

The early 19th century saw a pivotal moment in Australian history. In 1808, Governor William Bligh, appointed to address corruption and the illicit rum trade in the New South Wales Corps, faced resistance from officers involved in the lucrative rum business. The rebellion, later known as the Rum Rebellion, resulted in Bligh's deposition and marked a period of tumultuous governance.

While the rebellion wasn't directly related to rum production, it did contribute to a broader historical context of efforts to regulate and control alcohol consumption in the colony.

THE FIRST DISTILLERIES

The Beenleigh Distillery began its operations in 1884 in Eagleby, Queensland, marking the

THE FIRST FLEET
The First Fleet arrives in Botany Bay, Sydney, in 1788 in this painting by William Bradley.

BLIGH'S ARREST
A cartoon from 1810 shows the arrest of Governor Bligh. The Rum Rebellion was the only time in Australia's history that the government was overthrown by a military coup.

establishment of Australia's first licensed rum distillery. Legend has it that it was the successor to a floating moonshine distillery called the SS *Walrus*. The craft navigated along rivers between cane plantations in the early 19th century, producing illicit alcohol and evading authorities.

Four years later, in 1888, Bundaberg Rum was founded in Bundaberg, Queensland. A group of sugar millers who sought to find a profitable use for their molasses established the distillery and produced their first rum in 1889.

20TH AND 21ST CENTURIES

The early 20th century saw a decline in the Australian rum industry due to changing consumer preferences and economic challenges. Temperance advocates succeeded in having alcohol sales prohibited in the Federal Capital Territory (later the Australian

Capital Territory) from 1911 to 1928. Distilleries faced closures and only a handful survived.

In the late 20th and early 21st centuries, however, there has been a notable revival of interest in craft spirits and the rediscovery of traditional Australian rum. A new

generation of distillers has emerged, reviving the art of small-batch rum production. The increased interest in unique and artisanal products has contributed to the growth of boutique distilleries dedicated to crafting high-quality Australian rum.

CONTEMPORARY AUSTRALIAN RUM

The 21st century has seen a resurgence in the Australian rum scene, with a focus on craftsmanship, quality, and the unique flavours derived from local sugarcane. Distilleries such as Beenleigh and Husk have gained recognition for their premium rums. Husk has registered a trademark and a set of rules with IP Australia that define where and how rum can be made to be called Australian cultivated rum (ACR; see p174).

RUM IN AFRICA

Although sugarcane had been cultivated in Africa for hundreds of years, rum production and consumption were introduced primarily through European colonialism, particularly by the Portuguese, Dutch, British, French, and Spanish.

THE SPREAD OF RUM IN AFRICA

The colonial powers established sugar plantations in various parts of Africa, particularly in regions with favourable climates for sugarcane cultivation, such as the islands of Mauritius, Réunion, and Cape Verde, as well as parts of West Africa and Madagascar.

The transatlantic slave trade also played a significant role in the spread of rum within Africa. Rum was a key commodity exchanged for enslaved Africans, particularly as part of the triangular trade route between Europe, Africa, and the Americas (see pp30–31). Traders often acquired rum from European merchants in exchange for goods, which they then used as currency or to trade items in the interior of Africa.

While much of the rum consumed in Africa historically was imported from European colonies in the Caribbean or produced in Europe, some African countries also developed their own sugarcane spirit and rum production.

MAURITIUS

Rum production in Mauritius began during the colonial period using forced labour under Dutch, French, and British rule. The Dutch were the first to introduce sugarcane to Mauritius, in the mid-17th century, but it was during the French colonial period (1715–1810) that rum production grew significantly.

Distilleries were established across the island to process molasses into rum, which was mainly consumed locally as well as exported to other colonies in

TRADING POST
A woodcut from 1894 depicts a colonial trading post in the Upper Guinea region of West Africa.

BRITISH POSTER
A poster published by the British government's Empire Marketing Board in the 1930s promotes the sugar and rum products of Mauritius, then a British colony.

the Indian Ocean region. The first distillery was built by the governor-general, Mahé de La Bourdonnais, in 1740. By 1789, sugar plantations in Mauritius were producing 2.2 million litres (485,000 gallons) of rum annually. This figure dropped to 1.1 million litres (242,000 gallons) between 1801 and 1804 due to the French Revolutionary Wars (1792–1802).

After the British took control of the colony in 1810, local consumption dropped, but the export trade increased, albeit to different markets than when the island was controlled by the French. Madagascar, Seychelles, and the east coast of Africa were the prime destinations, as well as the new "motherland", Britain. By 1878, there were 37 rum distilleries operating on Mauritius.

By the 1890s, Mauritius vied for a top spot in the world rum trade, exporting an average of 3.8 million litres (836,000 gallons) a year. By 1914, at the outbreak of World War I, the 37 distilleries were producing approximately 5 million litres (1 million gallons) of rum.

The local population drank rum in the form of grog (rum diluted with water), called *topette*, but poor distillation led to an alcohol of inferior quality, and its popularity decreased over time. In 1933,

poorly distilled alcohol was banned on the island, with only the production of traditional rum made from molasses still allowed.

In 1968, Mauritius became independent from Britain, and rum producers imposed preferential tariffs on European countries for the export of rum, but the production of agricultural rum from cane juice was still banned. In 2006, the prohibition was lifted, even though the island was heavily

reliant on its sugar-refining industry. With the lifting of the ban came a minor explosion of the product, and Mauritius is now setting out its stall as a global provider of *rhum agricole* as well as traditional molasses rums.

Legally, it cannot use the words "*rhum agricole*" on its labels in the European markets, as this is a protected geographical indicator (GI) for rums made in the French Caribbean and Madeira.

SUGAR SALE
An engraving in the
Illustrated London News
of 16 February 1856
depicts the first sale
of sugar in the Cape
Colony in Durban's
market square.

SOUTH AFRICA

Rum production in the Natal region of South Africa can be traced back to the cultivation of sugarcane. Upon discovering the potential of molasses left over from the sugar boiling process, planters ventured into distillation. Among them was Thomas Reynolds of Oaklands Sugar Estate, situated near Chaka's Kraal. Renowned for his creation, dubbed "Umhlali water", Reynolds boldly advertised the quality of his product in the *Natal Mercury* newspaper in 1861, boasting his "Two Year Old Rum Equal to the finest Jamaica".

However, Reynolds' endeavours faced rigorous scrutiny from the Natal government's excise authorities, which proved stifling. In 1869, feeling constrained, he made the decision to liquidate his stock of the esteemed Colonial Rum (Umhlali water) and shutter his distillery. Nevertheless, the allure of rum production persisted, as others entered the fray.

A coarser variant, known as *gavine*, emerged. Evading excise duties, many engaged in illicit distribution on the black market. Consequently, illegally distilled *gavine* was widespread in Natal's shebeens, reflecting the resilience and adaptability of rum culture amid regulatory challenges.

ILLEGALLY DISTILLED *GAVINE*
FOUND WIDESPREAD AVAILABILITY
IN NATAL'S SHEBEENS.

GAVINE VS RUM

The South African government of the day was adamant that no unmatured spirit of this kind should be sold to customers as rum, which was seen as superior. So in 1913, the Union Parliament made it an offence to describe *gavine* and similar crude products as "rum". Instead, legal producers were authorized to market their product as cane spirit. These distillates were distributed to rum shops in 4-gallon (18-litre) glass jars, often at overproof strength. Shopkeepers diluted the cane spirit before selling it to customers.

It wasn't until the 1950s that efforts were made to introduce a recognized brand of cane spirit, exemplified by the creation of Mainstay. Despite this, throughout the 1980s, all domestically produced sugarcane distillates in South Africa were labelled as either "cane spirits" or simply referred to as "cane".

Meanwhile, the popularity of imported rum varieties among consumers surged, with local brands like Squadron Dark and imported brands such as Red Heart gaining traction, sometimes incorporating a blend that included Caribbean rum.

To address the growing demand and to distinguish between different spirits, the government implemented the Liquor Products Act 60 of 1989. It established guidelines to define the difference between cane spirit and rum.

Accordingly, cane spirits were required to be distilled in a rectifying or fractionating column with no particular colour, flavour, or aroma, resembling vodka. In contrast, South African rum could be produced using pot or column stills, but it must possess the distinctive taste and aroma characteristic of rum, clearly distinguishable from cane spirit or any other class of spirit.

Since 2010, there has been a steady supply of craft rum distilleries making authentic rum or producing rum brands. Today, brands like Tapanga, Mhoba, Copeland Rum, Hope Distillery, and the new Elephantom Rum are some of the torchbearers for the future of South African rum.

MAINSTAY
Launched in 1954, Mainstay cane spirit quickly became popular, becoming South Africa's top-selling spirit in the 1980s. It was discontinued in 2020.

HOW IS ----RUM---- MADE?

RUM, THE DISTILLED SPIRIT with a heritage deeply rooted in the Caribbean, is defined as a potently flavourful and diverse alcoholic beverage. Legally, rum must be made exclusively from sugarcane or its byproducts, such as molasses, sugarcane syrup, or fresh cane juice. However, the essence of true rum lies in the meticulous processes of fermentation, the art of distillation, maturation, *terroir*, and, more importantly, know-how. Rum embraces a spectrum of expressions, from light and crisp to rich and full-bodied. The ageing journey in oak barrels imparts nuanced complexities, infusing the spirit with notes of tropical spices and fruit. Rum is more than a drink – it is a cultural expression, a historical narrative, and a tantalizing voyage for the discerning palate.

THE ESSENCE OF RUM

In the world of spirits, rum stands as a testament to the marriage of nature's bounty and human ingenuity. Its genesis lies in fields of sugarcane, and its alchemical evolution is a symphony of time, craftsmanship, and the secrets held within each carefully chosen ingredient.

THE GREEN HEARTBEAT

At the core of every drop of rum is the essence of sugarcane (*Saccharum officinarum*), a tall, bamboo-like grass that pulses through most tropical regions' veins. In the intricate dance of

fermentation and distillation (see pp64–67), it is sugarcane that defines rum production. The diversity of sugarcane varieties contributes to the kaleidoscope of flavours found in different types of rum, from the light and floral to the rich and robust.

THE ESSENCE OF *TERROIR*

In the realms of *rhum agricole*, fresh sugarcane juice takes centre stage, offering a vibrant and grassy alternative to molasses-based counterparts. This ingredient, celebrated for its freshness and

SUGARCANE

With its luscious, green stalks and sweet sap, sugarcane is the fundamental ingredient, providing the fermentable sugar and raw material for making rum.

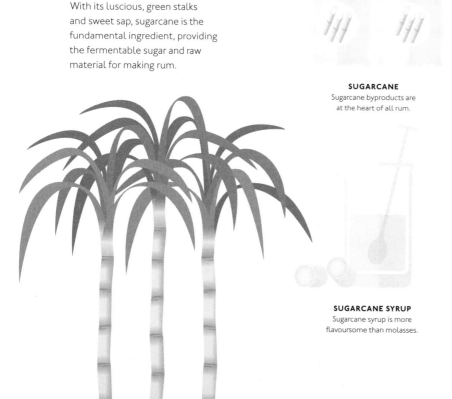

SUGARCANE
Sugarcane byproducts are at the heart of all rum.

SUGARCANE JUICE
Sugarcane juice is used to make *rhum agricole*.

SUGARCANE SYRUP
Sugarcane syrup is more flavoursome than molasses.

MOLASSES
Molasses is used to make the majority of rums.

RHUM AGRICOLE
Fresh sugarcane juice
is used to make *rhum
agricole*, such as these.

regional nuances, captures the essence of *terroir* – the unique environmental factors that influence the characteristics of the final product. Agricole rums showcase the diversity of sugarcane cultivars and the impact of microclimates on flavour profiles.

THE DARK ELIXIR

Derived from sugarcane, molasses is a rich, viscous byproduct of the sugar extraction process. This dark elixir is the cornerstone of many rum recipes, especially those crafted for depth and complexity. Molasses not only sweetens the fermenting mash but also imparts a robust character that becomes the canvas upon which the artistry of distillation is painted.

THE HONEY

Some rums use sugarcane syrup, also called sugarcane honey, a concentrated version of sugarcane juice that doesn't spoil as quickly. The honey is more flavoursome than molasses, as it has a higher concentration of fermentable sugars in it, and the resulting rums are normally more similar to molasses rums than they are to *rhums agricoles*.

MICROSCOPIC ALCHEMIST

Fermentation, the conversion of sugars into alcohol, relies on the presence of yeast. In the case of rum production, specific strains of yeast, such as *Saccharomyces cerevisiae*, are carefully selected to coax out desired flavours and aromas. This microscopic alchemist transforms the sugars into a vibrant wash or wine, laying the foundation for distillation.

WATER: A CRUCIAL ROLE

Simple yet indispensable, water plays a crucial role in the production of rum. Whether used in the fermentation process or to adjust the final proof of the spirit, water acts as the silent conductor in the symphony of flavours. In particular, Caribbean water, with its unique mineral composition, adds subtle nuances to the rum, contributing to its geographical identity.

TIME AND PATIENCE: THE UNSEEN INGREDIENTS

While not tangible, time and patience are integral elements in the recipe for exceptional rum. The ageing process (see pp76–77), during which the spirit slumbers in oak barrels, allows it to develop complexity, character, and depth. The interaction between the rum and the wood allows the spirit to absorb flavours from the barrel. The length of ageing varies, with some rums resting for only a year and others maturing for decades, each moment contributing to the flavour.

OAK BARREL
Ageing rums absorb flavours and texture from the barrel, such as vanilla, tannins, and caramel.

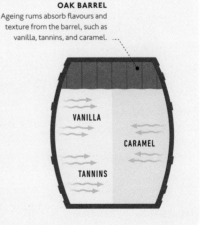

VANILLA

CARAMEL

TANNINS

FERMENTATION

In the journey from sugarcane to rum, fermentation is at the heart, converting sweet wine into a sugarcane alcohol. This alchemical process captures the essence of sugarcane, setting the stage for the rich tapestry of flavours that will define each bottle of rum.

MAKING THE WASH

At its core, fermentation is a biological marvel, where yeasts work their magic on the sugars present in sugarcane juice, syrup, or molasses. This is a crucial step in the rum-making process and gives birth to the wash, which is similar to a beer or wine. The wash is a raw, fermented alcoholic liquid, bubbling with carbon dioxide (CO_2).

As the wash ferments, it undergoes an evolution. The initial sweetness gives way to the heady aroma of alcohol, and subtle esters and congeners – chemical compounds responsible for flavour – begin to emerge.

After the chosen length of fermentation time, the wash can reach an alcoholic level of between 4% and 10% alcohol by volume (ABV), and it's this wash that will eventually be distilled into rum (see pp66–67).

FERMENTED WASH

This bubbling cauldron of potential, now transformed by fermentation, is ready for the next chapter in the tale of rum production.

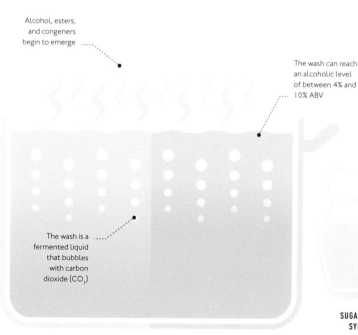

Alcohol, esters, and congeners begin to emerge

The wash can reach an alcoholic level of between 4% and 10% ABV

The wash is a fermented liquid that bubbles with carbon dioxide (CO_2)

SUGARCANE JUICE

MOLASSES

SUGARCANE SYRUP

THE LIVELY DANCE OF YEASTS TRANSFORMS THE COMPLEX SUGARS OF THE JUICE INTO ALCOHOL.

SUGARCANE JUICE: A GRASSY CONCERTO

In *rhum agricole* production (see p62–63), where it's all about the fresh sugarcane juice, fermentation begins almost immediately after extraction. The lively dance of yeasts, often indigenous to the distillery's environment, transforms the complex sugars of the juice into alcohol. This method, celebrated for its vibrancy and connection to *terroir*, yields rums with a grassy, floral character – an authentic expression of the sugarcane's regional identity.

MOLASSES: THE DARK RHYTHM

For rums crafted from molasses, the process of fermentation is equally mesmerizing. Molasses, a byproduct of sugarcane processing, is rich in sucrose, providing a fertile ground for fermentation. Some distilleries, such as Hampden Estate in Jamaica and Diamond Distillery in Guyana, carefully select yeast strains to infuse the wash with distinctive notes. This dark, treacle-like liquid evolves from its initial sweet viscosity to a wash of potential flavours.

WILD VS CONTROLLED FERMENTATION: THE ARTISTIC CHOICE

Both wild and controlled fermentation are valid expressions of the art of rum-making, contributing to the diverse palette of flavours within the world of rum.

- **WILD FERMENTATION** Some distilleries allow naturally occurring yeasts from the local environment to influence the process. This method imparts a unique fingerprint that links the rum to its surroundings.

- **CONTROLLED FERMENTATION** Controlled fermentation employs carefully selected yeast strains, providing a level of consistency and precision in flavour.

TIME AND TEMPERATURE: CONDUCTING COMPLEXITY

The amount of time the fermentation takes varies between distilleries. Shorter fermentations may result in lighter, fruitier rums, while longer fermentations extract deeper, more complex flavours.

Temperature also plays a role; some distillers allow natural environmental conditions to guide the fermentation process, while others meticulously control temperature to shape specific flavour profiles.

The interplay of time and temperature thus becomes an art, a delicate balance that ultimately defines the character of the rum.

DISTILLATION

Following on from fermentation, distillation now takes centre stage. It's a process that harnesses the principles of evaporation and condensation, and exploits the different boiling points of alcohol and water, allowing their separation to create a more concentrated and refined spirit.

LOADING THE STILL

After fermentation, when the yeast has stopped working or has died, the resulting "dead wash" is transferred to a still. This is often a pot still or column still (see pp68–71), depending on the distillery's preference and the desired characteristics of the final rum.

HEATING THE WASH

The still is heated to a controlled temperature, causing the alcohol in the dead wash to evaporate.

The different boiling points of alcohol and water are key to the separation of alcohol from the wash. Alcohol (ethanol) will start to boil at 78.3°C (173°F), while water boils at 100°C (212°F), so the alcohol evaporates before the water.

MAKING RUM

Rum undergoes a number of processes before the finished product is bottled.

STILL
Distillers may use a pot still or column still, or a combination of both

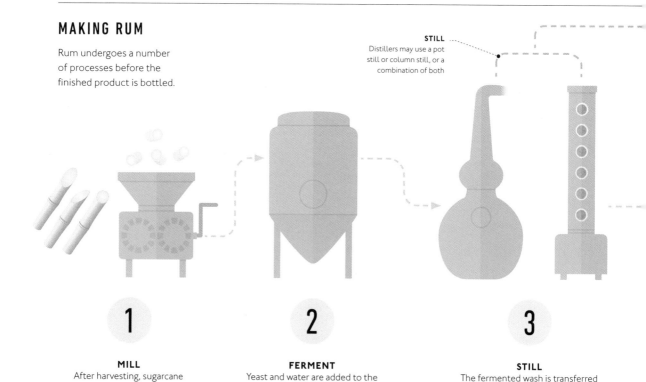

1

MILL
After harvesting, sugarcane is crushed by a machine to harvest the juice.

2

FERMENT
Yeast and water are added to the sugarcane juice, syrup, or molasses to create a wash, which is heated.

3

STILL
The fermented wash is transferred to a pot still or a column still, where it is heated.

VAPORIZATION

As the wash is heated, the alcohol in the liquid turns into vapour and rises through the neck of the pot or column of the still. This vapour contains the desired alcohol and aromatic compounds that contribute to the flavour profile of the rum.

Rum pot stills are known for producing more flavourful and robust spirits, while column stills are efficient for producing lighter and cleaner distillates.

CONDENSATION

The alcohol vapour then passes through a condenser, a coiled tube or a column with cooling elements, which causes the vapour to condense back into a liquid. This cooling is typically facilitated by running cold water through the condenser.

COLLECTION AND FRACTIONATION

The condensed liquid, now known as the distillate or "new-make spirit", is collected in a receiver. This initial collection contains a mixture of different components, including the "heads" (the early distillate that has undesirable compounds), the "heart" (the desired distillate that has the optimal flavours), and the "tails" (the late distillate that has heavier compounds).

The distiller carefully makes cuts to separate the heads and tails from the heart, collecting only the purest and most flavourful portion. This process, known as fractionation, is crucial in determining the quality and characteristics of the final rum.

REDISTILLATION

In some cases, distillers may redistil the heart cut to further refine and concentrate the desired flavours. This can occur in a second or multiple distillation runs, especially in countries like Jamaica that still employ the traditional double retort still (see p69), which essentially triple distils in one batch.

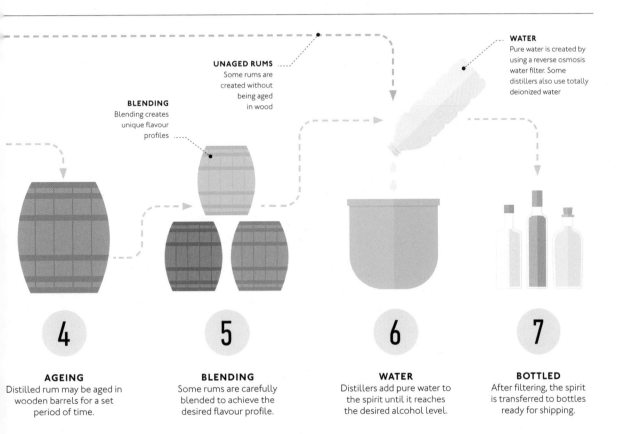

WATER
Pure water is created by using a reverse osmosis water filter. Some distillers also use totally deionized water

UNAGED RUMS
Some rums are created without being aged in wood

BLENDING
Blending creates unique flavour profiles

4

AGEING
Distilled rum may be aged in wooden barrels for a set period of time.

5

BLENDING
Some rums are carefully blended to achieve the desired flavour profile.

6

WATER
Distillers add pure water to the spirit until it reaches the desired alcohol level.

7

BOTTLED
After filtering, the spirit is transferred to bottles ready for shipping.

TYPES OF POT STILL

Revered for their artisanal approach, pot stills embrace the imperfections of the distillation process. They are often used in the production of superpremium and artisanal rums, allowing for greater control over the final product and capturing a wide range of flavours and aromas that define the rum's complexity.

ALEMBIC STILL

A historic and enduring fixture in rum production, the alembic still is a traditional pot still characterized by a copper pot and swan neck. The wash is heated in the pot, generating alcohol vapour that rises into the swan neck and is carried via the lyne arm to the condenser, where it becomes liquid again.

This batch distillation method, known for its simplicity and craftsmanship, allows the distiller to carefully select the optimal hearts during collection, ensuring the resulting rum embodies the rich and nuanced flavours derived from the sugarcane.

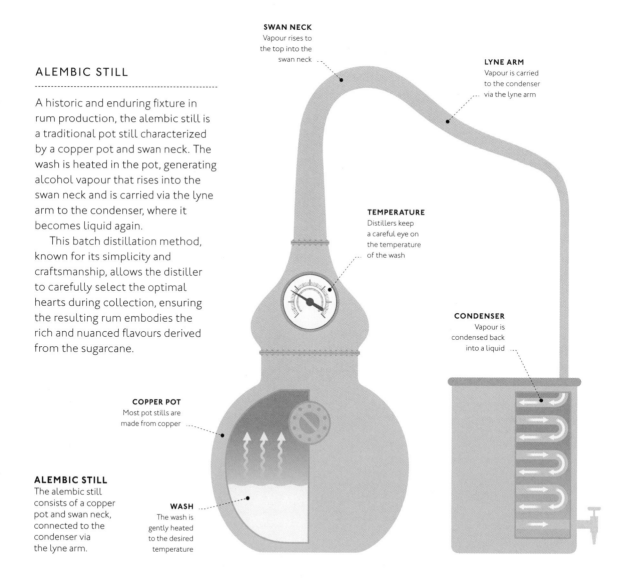

SWAN NECK
Vapour rises to the top into the swan neck

LYNE ARM
Vapour is carried to the condenser via the lyne arm

TEMPERATURE
Distillers keep a careful eye on the temperature of the wash

CONDENSER
Vapour is condensed back into a liquid

COPPER POT
Most pot stills are made from copper

ALEMBIC STILL
The alembic still consists of a copper pot and swan neck, connected to the condenser via the lyne arm.

WASH
The wash is gently heated to the desired temperature

DOUBLE RETORT STILL

The wash in the main kettle is heated until it reaches boiling point. Instead of proceeding to the condenser, the alcoholic vapour is directed through the lyne arm into the first retort. The vapour rises into the low wines (a distillate at about 30% ABV), where it condenses and becomes enriched with spirit, raising the ABV from 30% to about 60%. The heat generated from the first retort then vaporizes the liquid again, which moves into the second retort. Here, it bubbles in the high wines (a distllate at about 70% ABV). In this phase, vapour undergoes further alcohol enrichment before being distilled for a third time, reverting back to vapour and ultimately reaching the condenser, which yields the final rum.

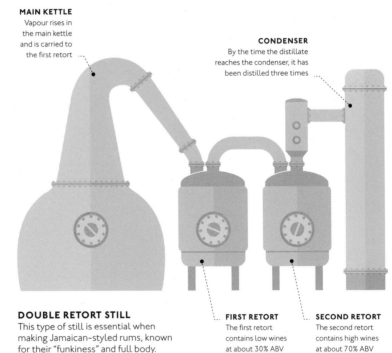

MAIN KETTLE
Vapour rises in the main kettle and is carried to the first retort

CONDENSER
By the time the distillate reaches the condenser, it has been distilled three times

DOUBLE RETORT STILL
This type of still is essential when making Jamaican-styled rums, known for their "funkiness" and full body.

FIRST RETORT
The first retort contains low wines at about 30% ABV

SECOND RETORT
The second retort contains high wines at about 70% ABV

HYBRID STILL

Some distilleries use a combination of pot and column sections, sometimes known as a hybrid still, to merge the flavour complexity of pot distillation with the efficiency of column distillation (see pp70–71).

Hybrid stills can be run as a simple pot still, a stripping still (used to strip the alcohol out of the initial wash quickly and efficiently), or as a column still.

Most have a three-way valve to control which section of the still the rum vapours travel through, allowing distillers to bypass any section they desire.

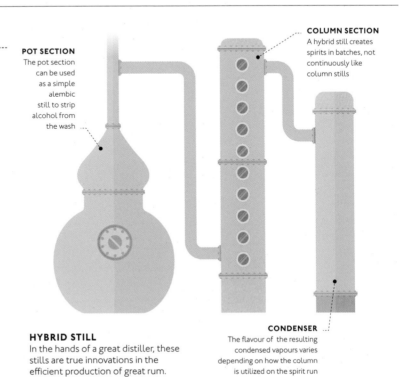

POT SECTION
The pot section can be used as a simple alembic still to strip alcohol from the wash

COLUMN SECTION
A hybrid still creates spirits in batches, not continuously like column stills

HYBRID STILL
In the hands of a great distiller, these stills are true innovations in the efficient production of great rum.

CONDENSER
The flavour of the resulting condensed vapours varies depending on how the column is utilized on the spirit run

TYPES OF COLUMN STILL

Rum makers began using column stills primarily for efficiency and consistency. They allow for continuous distillation, producing higher-proof alcohol more efficiently than traditional pot stills.

COFFEY STILL

The Coffey still, also known as a patent still, is a continuous distillation apparatus widely used in traditional rum production. It consists of two columns. The first column, the analyser, vaporizes the wash – typically molasses-based – in the presence of steam. The wash enters the first column, usually from the top or midsection, while steam is fed into the column from the bottom, travelling upwards and eventually coming into contact with the fermented wash.

As the vapour rises through the column, it makes contact with each successive plate, which purifies it. More volatile compounds continue upwards, while heavier, less volatile compounds reflux and fall down the column. The vapour then moves into the second column, known as the rectifier, where it undergoes further purification.

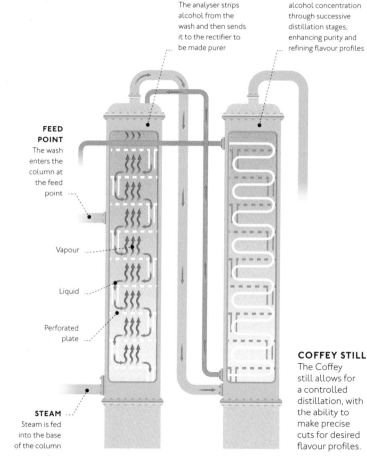

ANALYSER
The analyser strips alcohol from the wash and then sends it to the rectifier to be made purer

RECTIFIER
The rectifier optimizes alcohol concentration through successive distillation stages, enhancing purity and refining flavour profiles

FEED POINT
The wash enters the column at the feed point

Vapour

Liquid

Perforated plate

STEAM
Steam is fed into the base of the column

COFFEY STILL
The Coffey still allows for a controlled distillation, with the ability to make precise cuts for desired flavour profiles.

COPPER AND STAINLESS STEEL STILLS

Traditional pot stills are often made of copper, which interacts with the distillate, removing unwanted sulphurs and contributing to the development of complex flavours. Some column stills also have copper components.

A number of distilleries use stainless steel stills, which are easier to clean and maintain. While stainless steel doesn't interact with the distillate in the same way as copper, it's favoured for its durability and efficiency.

CREOLE STILL

From the second half of the 19th century, new distillation devices were introduced into the French Caribbean – in particular, a type of column still known as a Creole column still. The Creole still is synonymous with today's *rhum agricole* (see pp62–63).

Rums produced in the first imported columns were of extremely low quality, and the columns had to be adapted to the *rhum agricole* specifics. The usual two-column configuration was combined into a taller, single column, well suited to distilling at lower alcoholic strengths. The enrichment (rectification) plates were made larger, and the number of plates was reduced to increase the wash's exposure time to heat and metal, producing more esters essential to the *rhum* bouquet.

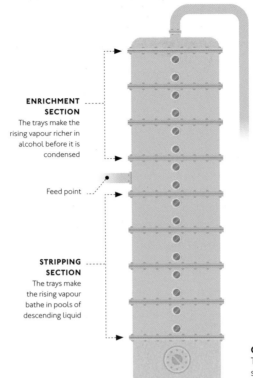

ENRICHMENT SECTION
The trays make the rising vapour richer in alcohol before it is condensed

Feed point

STRIPPING SECTION
The trays make the rising vapour bathe in pools of descending liquid

CREOLE STILL
The Creole column still was adapted to make *rhum agricole*.

MULTI-COLUMN STILL

Multi-column stills, prevalent in modern industrial rum production, feature several vertical columns. They enable a refined separation of alcohol and congeners, typically yielding lighter and cleaner spirits suitable for various styles, including unaged white and lightly aged rums.

The wash enters the top of the first column, called the analyser or beer column. As it falls down the column, it vaporizes as steam rises through the multiple trays. Each tray captures specific components based on their boiling points. The rising vapour, now enriched with alcohol and flavour compounds, moves through the extractive and rectification columns. These further refine the distillate, enhancing purity and removing undesirable elements.

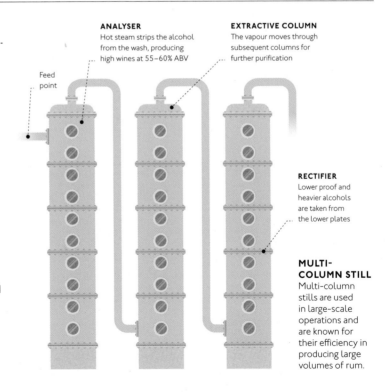

Feed point

ANALYSER
Hot steam strips the alcohol from the wash, producing high wines at 55–60% ABV

EXTRACTIVE COLUMN
The vapour moves through subsequent columns for further purification

RECTIFIER
Lower proof and heavier alcohols are taken from the lower plates

MULTI-COLUMN STILL
Multi-column stills are used in large-scale operations and are known for their efficiency in producing large volumes of rum.

THE BASE SPIRIT

Like all spirits, rum begins life as a transparent liquid when it emerges from a still. It is a pristine and unadulterated alcohol, capturing the essence of sugarcane or molasses in its purest form – "sugarcane *eau de vie*".

WHITE RUM

As the distillation process concludes, the resulting spirit, known as "new make", "*aguardiente*", or "white rum", is characterized by its clarity and transparency. There is a perceived sweetness in its taste, but it is not sugary sweet as the sugar molecules from the wash cannot pass on through distillation. This crystal-clear liquid holds within it the potential for diverse expressions and serves as a canvas for the skilled hands of the master blenders.

White rums are the foundation of all styles of rum. This absence of colour naturally distinguishes

WHITE RUM
Some white rums are unaged when bottled and sold.

white rum from its aged counterparts, allowing the drinker to witness the raw purity of the distillate. But despite its clear appearance, white rums are far from a blank slate. The journey through the still imparts a delicate, intricate complexity. The choice of distillation method can define the

rum's initial character: pot stills for boldness, roundness, and big, aromatic flavours; column stills for finesse, herbal notes, and light, fruity aromas; or a blend of both for a nuanced balance. These base spirits are rested, filtered, and blended, or just diluted with water to be aged or bottled.

SUGARCANE AND MOLASSES RUMS

For those clear rums crafted exclusively from sugarcane juice, the *terroir* of the sugarcane fields is vibrantly present. The climate, soil, and cultivation practices all leave their mark on the aromatic compounds and flavours within the white rum.

Molasses-based rums, on the other hand, generally carry the rich, robust essence of the sugarcane byproduct, often undergoing a meticulous fermentation process that contributes to the final profile.

RUM'S CHARACTER

The sugar source, type of fermentation, how it was distilled, and at what proof are all major factors in the character of a rum. And that's before the possibility of blending and ageing in wood, and before filtration to remove the colour and bring the rum back to water-white. So, for some white rums, the journey doesn't end with distillation. Master blenders may artfully combine spirits from different batches or distillation methods to achieve a final product that harmonizes the best qualities of each component. Distilleries across the Caribbean, from Jamaica to Puerto Rico, contribute their unique touch, whether through the use of traditional pot stills, modern column stills, or a blend of both.

Each distillery's approach imparts distinct regional characteristics, which may also be governed by local rules and regulations (see pp12–13) as to what defines a white rum.

SUGAR SOURCE
The sugar may come from sugarcane juice, sugarcane syrup, or molasses.

HOW IT'S DISTILLED
Each type of still contributes a different flavour profile to the rum.

RUM'S UNIQUE CHARACTER

A number of factors contribute to the making of a rum's unique character, including sugar source, fermentation, and type of still used.

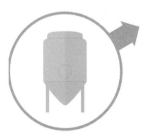

TYPE OF FERMENTATION
Fermentation may be short, long, controlled, or wild.

IS IT BLENDED?
Some rums are blended to create a unique flavour profile.

IS IT AGED IN WOOD?
The characteristics imparted to a rum depend on whether it's aged in wooden barrels.

RESTING RUM

Resting rum in wooden and stainless steel vats can impart different characteristics to the final product due to the interaction between the rum and the container.

WOODEN OR STAINLESS STEEL VAT?

The choice between wooden and stainless steel vats depends on the desired characteristics of the final rum. Distillers often choose wooden vats, usually made from oak, when the goal is to impart complex flavours and colours through interaction with the wood. They prefer stainless steel vats when the aim is to maintain the original characteristics of the distilled spirit.

Some rum producers may also use a combination of both types of vats for blending and achieving specific flavour profiles. In Martinique, for example, all white rums (rhums blancs) that comply with their appellation d'origine contrôlée (AOC) must be rested – usually in stainless steel tanks – for at least three months after distillation. If the rum is rested in oak, the resting cannot exceed three months.

WOODEN VAT

FLAVOUR INFUSION

When resting in wooden vats, the rum interacts with the wood, imparting flavours, aromas, and a little colour to the spirit. This process is influenced by compounds in the wood, such as tannins and lignin.

OXYGEN EXCHANGE

Wooden vats allow a slow and controlled exchange of oxygen between the environment and the rum. This interaction can contribute to the development of complex flavours and help mellow the spirit over time.

MATURATION

Rum ageing in wooden vats may undergo a maturation process, contributing to the overall character of the spirit. This maturation is often influenced by factors like temperature, humidity, and the size and age of the cask.

STAINLESS
STEEL VAT

THE CHOICE
BETWEEN
WOODEN AND
STAINLESS
STEEL VATS
DEPENDS ON
THE DESIRED
PROFILE
OF THE
FINAL RUM.

NEUTRAL ENVIRONMENT

Stainless steel vats provide a neutral environment that does not interact with the rum in terms of flavour or aroma. This is advantageous when the goal is to maintain the original characteristics of the spirit without any influence from the container.

TEMPERATURE CONTROL

Stainless steel vats don't let in any air, so they allow distillers to manage temperature conditions more effectively. Consistent temperature is crucial for achieving the desired ageing or resting effects in a rum.

CONSISTENT FLAVOUR

Stainless steel vats offer consistency in terms of ageing and storage conditions. Rum makers often use them in the production of light or white rums, or for large-scale production, where maintaining a consistent flavour profile across batches is a priority.

RESTING VS AGEING

It's important to note that resting is different from ageing (see pp76–77). Ageing typically involves the spirit being stored in smaller wooden barrels for an extended period, allowing it to mature and develop flavours from the wood.

AGEING RUM IN BARRELS

The practice of ageing rum in barrels has historical roots that likely evolved through experimentation and practical considerations.

THE BENEFIT OF BARRELS

In the early days of rum production, barrels were readily available and widely used for the transportation of goods, including alcoholic beverages. Rum makers observed that rum stored in wooden barrels underwent changes in flavour, colour, and aroma over time.

The use of barrels for ageing provides several benefits, including mellowing the harsh characteristics of raw rum, imparting flavour, and enhancing complexity (see right).

Over time, rum makers refined their techniques based on trial and error, as well as shared knowledge within the industry. As the positive effects of ageing in barrels became evident, it became a standard practice in rum-making.

Today, the art and science of rum production involve a combination of tradition, expertise, and innovation, with barrel ageing remaining a fundamental step in creating premium rums with distinctive flavour profiles.

FLAVOUR FROM THE BARRELS

Here are some of the most common flavours associated with rum ageing in wooden barrels:

VANILLA	CARAMEL	OAK	SPICE	TANNINS
Derived from the compound vanillin present in oak, vanilla is a hallmark flavour in many aged rums. It adds sweetness and richness to the spirit.	Ageing in charred barrels (see pp80–81) leads to the extraction of caramelized sugars, imparting a sweet and toasty or toffee-like flavour to the rum.	Wood contributes flavours like oak, providing structure and depth. This can range from subtle woody notes to more pronounced oakiness.	Aged rums often showcase spicy notes, like hints of cinnamon or clove, which develop due to the interaction between the spirit and the wood.	Tannins from the wood contribute to mouthfeel, imparting a dryness and astringency that can enhance the overall balance of the spirit.

WHY ARE RUMS AGED?

Although not all rums are aged, there are a number of advantages to ageing rum.

FLAVOUR DEVELOPMENT
The rum interacts with the wood, extracting flavours and compounds, such as vanilla, caramel, and oak.

COLOUR ENHANCEMENT
The interaction with the wood imparts a rich, amber hue to the rum. The longer the ageing process, the darker the rum.

AROMA IMPROVEMENT
The air inside the barrel promotes oxidation and the aroma profile evolves, adding depth and character.

REFINEMENT
Ageing helps to mellow and smooth out the edges, allowing the rum to achieve a more refined and mature character.

BALANCE AND HARMONY
Ageing contributes to the overall balance and harmony of the flavours, creating a well-rounded drink.

DISTINCTIVE FLAVOURS
Barrels that previously held other alcohol, such as whisky, impart unique flavours and characteristics to the rum.

MARKET PREFERENCES
Aged rums are often seen as higher quality by connoisseurs. Ageing allows rum makers to create premium products.

NON-AGED RUMS
Not all rums undergo extensive ageing. Some lighter styles of rum may not be aged for an extended period and are often bottled shortly after distillation. The decision on ageing depends on the desired style of rum and the preferences of the rum maker.

FRUIT	CHOCOLATE	SPICY OAK	LEATHERY OR TOBACCO	MOLASSES RICHNESS
epending on the ype of wood and the geing conditions, ms may develop uity notes, such as ried fruits, raisins, or ark fruit flavours.	Some aged rums exhibit chocolatey notes, ranging from milk to dark chocolate, adding a layer of complexity and sweetness.	Beyond individual spice notes, the overall influence of spicy oak can be present, providing a warm and nuanced character to the rum.	In certain aged rums, you may find leathery or tobacco-like notes, adding a layer of earthiness and complexity.	For rums made from molasses, the ageing process can enhance the molasses-derived richness, contributing to a more rounded and full-bodied profile.

MATURATION AND THE ANGELS' SHARE

While ageing is a crucial component, maturing denotes a comprehensive and nuanced approach to the rum's overall improvement. It includes factors beyond barrel ageing, such as blending, environmental conditions, and overall refinement.

AGEING VS MATURING

Ageing in rum specifically refers to the time spent in wooden barrels (see pp76–77), where the spirit undergoes transformative interactions with the wood. Maturing encompasses the entire developmental journey from distillation to bottling.

TROPICAL AGEING

Tropical ageing in rum is a distinctive maturation process that occurs in regions with warm and humid climates, such as the Caribbean. The higher temperatures cause the spirit to expand and contract within the barrels more rapidly, intensifying the extraction of flavours from the wood and resulting in a more dynamic and robust flavour profile. Rum in Jamaica, for example, can age three times faster than Scotch whisky.

THE ANGELS' SHARE

The tropical climate also promotes greater evaporation, known as the "angels' share", concentrating the remaining liquid and enhancing its complexity. In Scotland, as whisky ages in oak barrels, a portion of the spirit evaporates through the porous wood. This loss, the angels' share, is often around 2 per cent or more per year. In Kentucky, in the United States, bourbon whiskey loses between 2 and 5 per cent of its volume a year to the said angels. While in Jamaica, rum ageing in an oak barrel could lose from 4 to 6 per cent of its volume per year (see below). In Jamaica, the angels' share is called the duppy share.

AGEING IN THE TROPICS

Spirits experience greater evaporation in tropical climates compared to those that are aged in more temperate climates.

Loss due to evaporation

SCOTCH WHISKY

2% loss per year

KENTUCKY BOURBON

2–5% loss per year

JAMAICAN RUM

4–6% loss per year

IN JAMAICA, THE ANGELS' SHARE IS
CALLED THE DUPPY SHARE, NAMED AFTER
A SUPERNATURAL ENTITY OR SPIRIT.

HUMIDITY

The level of humidity plays a
crucial role in determining the
evaporation of water and alcohol
from barrels, influencing the proof
(ABV) of the spirit. In regions with
high humidity, such as the
production areas of Scotch,
Cognac, and many rums, a greater
proportion of alcohol evaporates
compared to water. Consequently,
the proof of the spirit decreases as
it ages. In drier climates, such as
Kentucky where American whiskey
is primarily produced, more water
evaporates from the barrels,
causing the proof to increase.

DOUBLE AGEING

The terms "double ageing" or
"double maturation" typically refer
to a process in which the distilled
rum undergoes ageing in two
separate barrels or casks. This
method is employed to enhance
and refine the flavours of the rum.

The first stage usually takes
place in traditional oak barrels.
During this initial ageing process,
the rum absorbs more of its final
flavour from the wood.

DOUBLE AGEING

Rum makers double age their rum to give
it a unique and desired flavour profile.

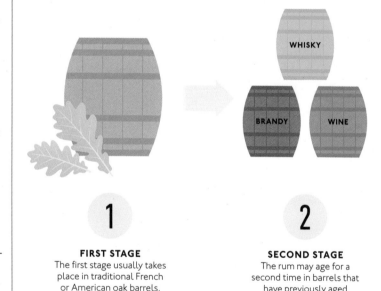

1

FIRST STAGE
The first stage usually takes
place in traditional French
or American oak barrels.

2

SECOND STAGE
The rum may age for a
second time in barrels that
have previously aged
another product.

The rum is then transferred to a
second set of barrels. These could
be made from a different type of
wood or have previously been
used for ageing another product,
such as whisky, brandy, or wine.
This secondary ageing imparts
additional complexity and depth
to the rum, allowing it to absorb
different flavours and characteristics.

CHARRING THE BARRELS

Charring, or toasting, barrels significantly impacts the flavours, aromas, and overall character of the rum. There are several primary reasons why rum makers choose to char barrels.

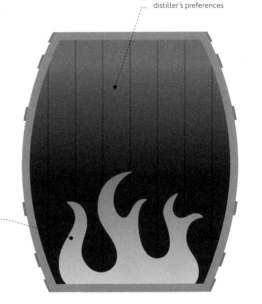

CHAR LEVEL
The intensity of the charring varies according to the distiller's preferences

CHARRING
Barrels are usually charred by applying heat to the inside of the barrel

WHY CHAR BARRELS?

Charring the inside of barrels is a skilled technique that rum makers use to influence the character of the final aged product. Charring imparts flavour, sweetness, and depth to the rum, helps to remove undesirable compounds, enhances the colour of the rum, and adds aromatic depth and character (see below).

THE EFFECTS OF CHARRING

Rum that is aged in charred barrels undergoes a number of desirable processes that influence the quality of the final rum.

FLAVOUR INFUSION	CARAMELIZATION	REMOVING UNDESIRABLE COMPOUNDS	ENHANCED COLOUR EXTRACTIO
Charring opens up the wood's pores, breaking down compounds such as cellulose, hemicellulose, and lignin, and so imparting flavours such as vanilla, caramel, nuttiness, leather, spice, and smoke.	Charring can lead to caramelization of the wood sugars. This process imparts sweetness and depth to the rum, contributing to the development of rich and complex flavour notes.	Undesirable compounds in the wood, such as harsh tannins and bitter elements, can be removed by charring. Unwanted flavours are eliminated, creating a more refined spirit.	Charring enhances the extraction of colour from th wood, resulting in a deeper and richer hue for the aged rum. The caramelized sugars and compounds released during charring contribute to the final colour of the spirit.

CHARRING LEVELS

The choice of charring level is a key element of a distillery's craftsmanship, allowing for the creation of unique and distinctive rums. The char levels refer to the degree to which the interior of the barrel is charred during the coopering process. These various char levels impart different flavours and characteristics to the aged rum.

The choice of char level allows rum makers to tailor the ageing process to achieve specific flavour profiles. Lighter chars may be preferred for rums that undergo shorter maturation. Heavier chars, including the alligator char (see right), are often chosen for premium and long-aged expressions, with an emphasis on smokiness, depth, and complexity.

LIGHT CHAR: LEVEL 1
This level imparts subtle flavours and allows for a gentler interaction between the rum and the wood. It is often associated with a shorter ageing process.

MEDIUM CHAR: LEVEL 2 OR 3
Charring penetrates the wood more deeply, contributing more pronounced flavours of caramel, vanilla, and oak.

HEAVY CHAR: LEVEL 4 OR 5
This level imparts robust and complex flavours to the rum, including caramelization and smokiness. Heavy char barrels are often used for longer ageing.

ALLIGATOR CHAR
The term "alligator char" refers to the appearance of the charred wood, which is like the skin of an alligator. This very heavy char imparts bold and intense flavours.

AROMA DEVELOPMENT	IMPROVED MOUTHFEEL	ACCELERATED AGEING	CUSTOMIZATION AND CONTROL
Volatile compounds from the wood are released, influencing the aroma of the rum. This aromatic complexity adds depth and character to the spirit, with notes ranging from vanilla and spice to smoky and toasty elements.	Charring can impact the mouthfeel of the rum by introducing compounds that enhance texture and smoothness, such as lactones. These contribute to a more enjoyable and well-rounded spirit.	Charring can accelerate the ageing process. This is significant in regions with a shorter maturation period, as it allows the rum to achieve a desired level of complexity in a shorter time.	Different levels of charring or toasting can result in varying degrees of flavour intensity, allowing for a range of expressions within a distillery's portfolio.

TYPES OF BARREL

The type of barrel used to age rum can significantly influence the flavour, aroma, and overall character of the final spirit. While oak barrels are the most common choice, the specific type of oak, the size of the barrel, and whether it's new or used all play crucial roles.

CHOOSING BARRELS

The choice of barrel type is a critical decision made by rum producers, and it significantly influences the final flavour profile of the aged rum. Distillers may also use a combination of different barrels or employ various finishing techniques to create unique and complex expressions of their rums.

BARRELS THAT HAVE PREVIOUSLY BEEN USED TO AGE BOURBON ARE A POPULAR CHOICE FOR RUM AGEING.

CALVADOS CASKS

Casks from reputable Calvados producers in Normandy, France, are in high demand for rum blenders – the French oak that previously matured the apple brandy for several years is perfect for older rums.

AMERICAN OAK BARRELS

Barrels made from American white oak (*Quercus alba*) are widely used in the rum industry. These barrels are known for imparting flavours like vanilla, caramel, and sometimes a hint of coconut.

MADEIRA CASKS

Madeira casks, used for finishing or ageing, can introduce distinct wine-like and oxidative notes to rum, adding complexity to the final product.

WINE CASKS

Casks from various wine regions, such as red wine or white wine casks, can be used to age or mature rums. The choice of wine cask can influence the rum with wine-related flavours.

PORT WINE CASKS
Casks that previously held port wine can contribute fruity and sweet notes to rum. Port cask finishing is a technique employed by some distillers to impart these unique characteristics.

FRENCH OAK BARRELS
Usually made from common oak (*Quercus robur*) or sessile oak (*Q. petraea*), and often sourced from Limousin or Allier in France, these impart more nuanced spice, floral, and light, fruity notes to the rum than American oak.

BOURBON BARRELS
Ex-bourbon barrels are a popular choice for rum ageing. The residual flavours from the bourbon, including vanilla and caramel, can enhance the rum's complexity.

SHERRY CASKS
Casks that once held sherry can bring unique fruity, nutty, and sometimes raisin-like flavours to the rum. Sherry casks are often used for finishing or additional ageing and maturation to add layers of complexity.

COGNAC CASKS
Casks that previously housed Cognac can impart rich, fruity, and sometimes floral characteristics to rum. These casks are predominantly made from French oak.

NEW OAK BARRELS
Barrels made from new oak are less common in rum maturation due to the strong influence of the wood. Some distillers use new oak to impart more intense flavours, then transfer the rum to an older, used barrel.

HYBRID BARRELS
Some producers experiment with using barrels made from a combination of different types of wood, or barrels that were previously used for ageing multiple types of spirits. These hybrid barrels can contribute a wide range of flavours.

BLENDING RUM

Blending involves the combination of different aged rums to achieve a desired flavour profile, consistency, and balance. The art of blending requires expertise, sensory evaluation, and an understanding of the characteristics of various rums.

THE ART OF BLENDING

Blending is a multifaceted process that combines science, artistry, and tradition. It allows rum makers to influence their final product in a number of ways. The skilful art of blending is a hallmark of premium rum production, resulting in a wide array of distinctive and enjoyable spirits. Distillers blend rums for a variety of reasons.

DIVERSITY OF DISTILLATES

Rum production involves a range of raw materials, fermentation techniques, and distillation methods, leading to a broad spectrum of flavour profiles. Blending allows rum makers to harness the diverse qualities of these distillates, creating a final product that is greater than the sum of its parts.

In Jamaica, for example, the different types of rums are called marques (marks). These refer to distinct flavour profiles and production methods, resulting in unique rums (see p89).

CONSISTENCY

Blending is a means to achieve consistency in flavour, aroma, and colour across batches and bottles. Each barrel of aged rum can develop unique characteristics during the ageing process. By blending different barrels, distilleries can smooth out variations, ensuring that each bottle of the same rum maintains a consistent and recognizable quality. In some cases, a touch of caramel (burnt sugar) is added to some batches for consistency of colour only, not for sweetening.

BALANCING FLAVOURS

Blending enables rum makers to balance the flavour profile of the final product. Some rums may be characterized by intense

---

WHY ARE RUMS BLENDED?

There are a number of reasons why distillers choose to blend their rums.

HARNESS THE DIVERSITY OF DISTILLATES	CUSTOMIZE EXPRESSIONS
ENSURE CONSISTENCY	MEET MARKET PREFERENCES
BALANCE FLAVOURS	ADDRESS ECONOMIC CONSIDERATIONS
EXPRESS AGE	MAINTAIN QUALITY CONTROL
MANAGE WOOD INFLUENCES	UPHOLD TRADITIONAL PRACTICES
RECTIFY IMPERFECTIONS	ADAPT TO MARKET TRENDS

AGED RUMS
Age claims for Jamaican and Guyanese rums must designate the youngest rum.

RECTIFYING IMPERFECTIONS
Not every barrel of rum turns out as expected. Some may develop off-flavours or other imperfections during ageing. Blending allows rum makers to rectify these issues by combining rums with complementary qualities, smoothing out rough edges and enhancing positive attributes.

sweetness, while others may have more robust spiciness or oaky notes. Through meticulous blending, distillers can create a harmonious and well-rounded flavour profile that appeals to a wide range of palates.

AGE EXPRESSION
Many premium rums are blends of rums of different ages. Blending allows rum makers to achieve a desired level of maturity and complexity by combining younger, more vibrant rums with older, more nuanced ones. Some countries stipulate that the age statement on a rum label should refer to the youngest rum in the blend (see p92).

WOOD INFLUENCE
Rums aged in barrels absorb flavours from the wood (see pp76–77), and blending provides an opportunity to balance the impact of different barrels. For example, a rum aged in an intensely charred barrel may contribute more smoky and

woody notes, while a rum aged in a less charred barrel may bring forward subtler flavours. Blending allows for the careful management of these wood influences.

BALANCING FLAVOURS

Blending rums can balance out the flavour profile of a rum, creating a well-rounded product.

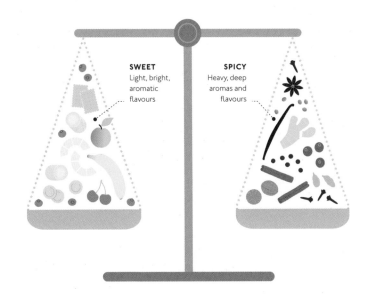

SWEET Light, bright, aromatic flavours

SPICY Heavy, deep aromas and flavours

BLENDING ALLOWS PRODUCERS TO ADAPT TO CHANGING CONSUMER PREFERENCES AND MARKET TRENDS.

CUSTOMIZATION

Blending provides rum makers with a tool for creativity and innovation. Distillers can experiment with different combinations of rums to create unique expressions that stand out in the market. This customization allows for the development of limited editions, special releases, or signature blends that showcase the distillery's craftsmanship (see below).

ECONOMICS OF AGEING

Ageing rum is a time-consuming process, and certain economic considerations, such as labour costs and adequate storage space, come into play. Blending allows distillers to maximize the use of aged stocks, optimizing the maturation process and releasing products with desirable qualities, without waiting for every barrel to reach the desired age.

QUALITY CONTROL

Rigorous quality control is essential in rum production. Blending provides an opportunity for sensory evaluation at various stages, allowing the distiller to assess the development of flavours and aromas. This ensures that only high-quality rums are selected for blending, maintaining the reputation of the brand.

TRADITIONAL PRACTICES

Blending has been a part of traditional rum-making practices for centuries. Master blenders often inherit knowledge and skills from previous generations, preserving the artistry and maintaining the consistency of well-established brands.

MARKET TRENDS

The rum market is dynamic, with trends evolving over time. Some drinkers prefer sweetened, dessert-like rums, while others prefer drier or more robust expressions. Blending allows producers to adapt to changing consumer preferences and market trends by creating new expressions or adjusting existing ones. It's at the blending stage that some rum brands, if legally permitted (see p93), add sugars to sweeten their rums.

CUSTOMIZED RUM

Produced in Barbados, Equiano Rum is a blend of rum from Mauritius aged in ex-Cognac casks and Barbadian rum aged in ex-bourbon barrels.

MAURITIAN RUM
aged in ex-Cognac casks

BARBADIAN RUM
aged in ex-bourbon barrels

SOLERA BLENDING

In *solera* blending, the oldest rums are in the
bottom row of barrels, with the youngest on the
top. A portion of the oldest rums is removed each
year for bottling, and rum from the rows above
partially refills the barrels on the rows below.

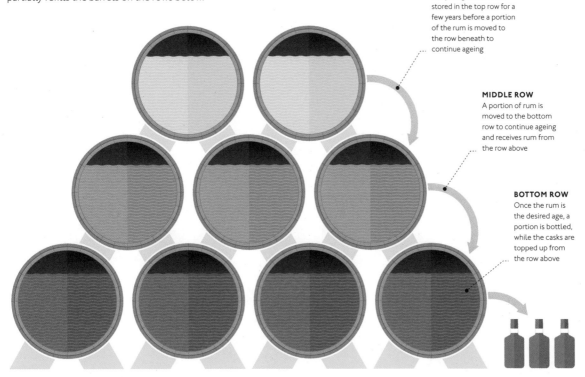

TOP ROW
The youngest rums are
stored in the top row for a
few years before a portion
of the rum is moved to
the row beneath to
continue ageing

MIDDLE ROW
A portion of rum is
moved to the bottom
row to continue ageing
and receives rum from
the row above

BOTTOM ROW
Once the rum is
the desired age, a
portion is bottled,
while the casks are
topped up from
the row above

SOLERA BLENDING

Solera blending is a dynamic
and continuous ageing process
commonly used in the production
of certain rums, especially in
countries like Guatemala and
Panama or other countries that
have a historical link to Spain.

Originating from the world of
sherry production, the *solera*
system involves stacking multiple
rows of barrels, with the oldest
barrels at the bottom and newer
ones stacked above. The term
"*solera*" – "on the ground" in
Spanish – refers to the lowest tier.

Each year, a fraction of the
oldest rum is removed from the
bottom row for bottling, and the
barrel is then partially refilled with
rum from the row above. Rum is
moved in the same way from the
upper rows. This cascading process
continues, creating a perpetual
blend that incorporates elements
from various age levels.

When done correctly, *solera*
blending imparts complexity,
consistency, and a harmonious
character to the final product,
as the older rums influence and
enhance the younger ones.

JAMAICAN RUM

Jamaican rum is renowned for its bold and robust profile, often characterized by rich flavours of tropical fruits, molasses, citrus peel, and spices.

THE FLAVOUR PROFILE

Rum from Jamaica carries a distinctive funkiness known as "*hogo*", derived from prolonged fermentation with dunder and muck (see right) and its double retort pot still distillation. With its complex aromas, Jamaican rum is beloved for its depth, intensity, and unmistakable Caribbean character.

THE JAMAICAN WAY

Molasses, yeast, filtered limestone water, and the "secret sauce" of dunder and sometimes muck undergo a prolonged fermentation. This develops unique acidic flavours ready to be crafted in pot stills. In some cases, traditional column stills are also used and blended with the pot still rums.

WHAT IS DUNDER?

Dunder is primarily the residue left in the still after a distillation run. It's a crucial element in the production of Jamaica rum, used to enhance flavour and character. Distilleries often collect and recycle dunder, incorporating it into subsequent fermentation batches. It's rich in organic matter, spent yeast, and various microorganisms, contributing to the development of complex and unique flavours in the rum.

WHAT ARE MUCK PITS?

Jamaican muck pits, also known as "dunder pits", are integral to traditional Jamaican rum production. These pits are large fermentation vessels filled with organic matter like cane juice residue, old fruits, spent wash, and bacteria-rich muck. Over time, this mixture undergoes natural fermentation, producing intense flavours and volatile compounds. Muck pits contribute to the characteristic funkiness and complexity of Jamaican rum, infusing it with unique aromas and flavours. Jamaican distilleries that still employ this method carefully manage and recycle muck pits, using them to inoculate new fermentation batches and maintain consistency in their rums.

TYPICAL JAMAICAN RUMS
Jamaican rums have varying aroma and flavour profiles, ranging from fruity and floral to rich and funky.

JAMAICAN "FUNK"

The signature "funk" associated with Jamaican rum is strongly connected with rums made in Trelawny, a parish in the north of the island. Rums made there are high in esters and have cult status, like Islay single malt whisky, boasting big, robust, fruity, and smoky flavours.

1
MOLASSES, WATER, AND YEAST
The wash is left to ferment naturally in open wooden vats for weeks, adopting the natural microclimate.

2
DUNDER AND MUCK
Dunder and sometimes muck from a pit or fermented cane juice vinegar are added to the wash during fermentation.

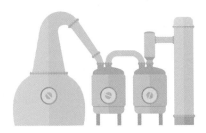

3
DISTILLATION
Distillation occurs in double retort pot stills, which enables a triple distillation in one pass. This also concentrates the natural flavours and esters that develop during the long fermentation.

4
UNIQUE MARQUES
A distillery creates a marque (see below) depending on the recipe of yeast, fermentation, distillation, and ageing.

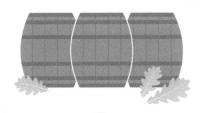

5
AGEING, BOTTLING, AND EXPORTING
The rums are then either matured in white oak barrels, or bottled unaged and exported.

TROPICAL AGEING

A tropical ageing process in oak barrels enhances character and increases the esters (flavour compounds) in the rum. The master blender skilfully blends different batches, creating a balanced and flavourful spirit with the distinctive, traditional richness and intensity of Jamaican rum.

JAMAICAN RUM MARQUES

Jamaican rum marques are specific styles or types of rum produced by individual distilleries on the island. Each marque has a letter code and is characterized by unique fermentation, distillation, and ageing techniques, resulting in unique flavour profiles. Marques also vary in esters, which contribute to the rum's aroma and flavour. Esters are formed throughout the rum-making process but are more notable in "high-ester" Jamaican rums, especially when compared to other styles. The marque DOK (Dermot Owen Kelly) from Hampden Estate has one of the highest ester levels in a rum.

CUBAN RUM

Based on the volumes sold, Cuban rum, or rum made the "Cuban way", is by far the most popular style of rum in the world.

CUBAN RUMS
Cuban rums typically have a light, dry, and refined profile that distinguishes them from other rums made in the Caribbean.

THE FLAVOUR PROFILE

Cuban rums are not like the pot-stilled, high-ester, or heavy rums associated with Jamaica or Guyana. Nor are they as grassy or vegetal as medium- to heavy-bodied *rhums* from Martinique or Guadeloupe. Cuban rum leans towards a light, dry, and refined profile that has historically influenced rums from the Dominican Republic, many countries in Central America, and Puerto Rico.

HOW IS IT MADE?

The art of rum making the Cuban way, the know-how, is a skill passed down from generation to generation by the *maestros roneros cubanos* (Cuban master blenders). Multiple styles of rums, called bases, are blended and aged in very old American oak barrels, which impart subtle woody notes to the maturing rum, rather than the heavy vanilla and tannins that would be present in new or first-filled ex-bourbon barrels.

AGUARDIENTE AND *REDISTILADO*

Today's rum from Cuba is still made in the traditional way with two types of rum and double ageing (see p 79). Cuban rum uses two different types of column distillate. The first is called *aguardiente* – Spanish for "fire water". This fiery spirit is around 75% ABV and is oily, savoury, and viscous with aromas of sugarcane, brine, green olives, and peppers.

The second distillate, called *redistilado* or *destilado de caña*,

THE CUBAN WAY

Blending to create a base is a unique characteristic of Cuban rums.

2 YEARS

1

AGEING THE AGUARDIENTE
The *aguardiente* is aged for a minimum of two years in old white oak barrels.

TODAY'S RUM FROM CUBA IS MADE WITH TWO TYPES OF RUM AND DOUBLE AGEING.

is re-distilled several times in a multi-column still to just under 96% ABV. This lighter spirit is subtle with hints of citrus oil and orchard fruits. Both the *aguardiente* and *redistilado* legally cannot be called rum at this stage because both are unaged spirits – by law, Cuban rums need to be aged for a minimum of two years.

AGUARDIENTE

REDISTILADO

75% ABV

96% ABV

TWO TYPES OF DISTILLATE
Cuban rum uses two types of column distillate, which have different alcoholic strengths.

CREATING A BASE

To make the distillates into Cuban-style rum, the *aguardiente* is aged for a minimum of two years and then filtered. It's then blended with the unaged *redistilado* and some old rum to create a "base" rum. Depending on the purpose of the rum and the requirements of the *maestro ronero*, the ratio of aged rum to *redistilado* in the blend varies. This style of blending is unique to the Cuban style of rums that we have available on our shelves (see pp138–41).

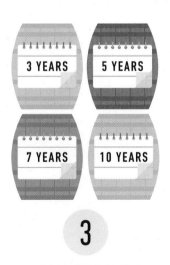

3 YEARS   5 YEARS

7 YEARS   10 YEARS

2

FILTERING AND BLENDING
The aged rum is filtered and blended with the *redistilado* and some old rum to create a base.

3

AGEING THE BASE
The base is then aged for a number of years – 3, 5, 7, or 10 – depending on the desired style of rum.

4

BLENDING AND BOTTLING
The aged bases are blended ready for bottling.

DECIPHERING RUM LABELS

Deciphering a rum label can be an enlightening experience for enthusiasts and newcomers alike, offering valuable insights into the spirit's origin, production methods, and flavour profile.

WHAT'S ON THE LABEL?

Besides the obvious colour reference of white, gold, or dark, a typical rum label contains key information that provides a snapshot of what to expect from the contents of the bottle.

1. BRAND NAME
The brand name, usually prominently displayed on the label, shows the company or distillery that produced the rum. Recognizable brands often signify quality and consistency, although craft producers may offer unique and innovative expressions.

2. COUNTRY OF ORIGIN
The label should specify the country where the rum was produced. Different regions have their own traditions and regulations that govern rum production and influence the style of the spirit.

3. DISTILLATION METHOD
Some labels may mention the distillation method used to produce the rum, such as pot or column stills. The words "pure single" mean the rum is pot distilled and from a single distillery, not blended with rums from another source or adulterated with sugar or spices (see box right).

4. AGEING STATEMENT
If the rum has been aged in wood, the label may include an ageing statement indicating the duration of maturation. In some countries, such as Jamaica, Barbados, and Cuba, the law states that only the youngest rum in the blend can be declared on the label. Other countries allow the average age or the oldest rum in their blend as their age statement, such as *solera*-aged rum (see p87).

1

4

5

NINEFOLD

CASK AGED
PURE SINGLE RUM

70 CL ℮   AUTHENTIC POT DISTILLED
SCOTTISH RUM   45% VOL

2

3

5. ALCOHOL CONTENT

All rums must state their alcohol content, either as percentage of alcohol by volume (ABV) or, in the United States, as degrees of proof, which is twice the ABV figure. Some countries have a minimum alcohol content for the spirit to be legally called a rum.

6. OFFICIAL SEAL OR LOGO

Many regulatory bodies use an official seal or logo that signifies the rum's geographical indication (GI) or protected denomination

of origin (PDO). It may include specific symbols or wording that denote the region of production, like Martinique's *appellation d'origine contrôlée* (AOC) or Cuba's *sello de garantía* (seal of guarantee). These certify the rum's authenticity, quality, and adherence to traditional production methods.

7. ADDITIVES AND FLAVOURINGS

Any flavourings or sweeteners should be disclosed on the label, like the word "spice". In the European Union (EU), rum

can be sweetened to up to 20g (³⁄₄oz) of sugar per litre (1 ¾ pints). Any more than this, and the label must legally say "spirit drink", which also applies to spiced rums (see pp20–21) bottled at less than 37.5% ABV.

ADDITIONAL DESCRIPTORS

Additional descriptors or marketing terms, like "single estate", "small batch", or "artisanal", suggest a more hands-on and limited production process, potentially resulting in a unique and carefully crafted rum.

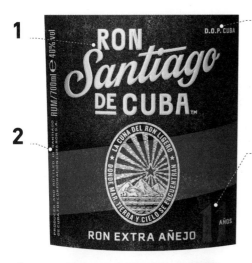

1

2

4

6

PDO
Cuba is this rum's protected denomination of origin

SPIRIT DRINK
These words also highlight that legally this is not a rum

7

THE GARGANO SYSTEM

The Gargano system, named after rum collector Luca Gargano, is a system for craft rums that emphasizes transparency and quality. It categorizes rum into four main groups.

- **PURE SINGLE RUM/*AGRICOLE***
  Pure single rums are made from a single distillery's pot still and are not blended with rums from other sources.

- **TRADITIONAL RUM**
  Traditional rums are distilled from a traditional Coffey or Creole column still.

- **AGRICULTURAL RUM**
  Agricultural rum, also known as *rhum agricole*, is made exclusively from fresh sugarcane juice. It is typically produced in French-

speaking Caribbean islands like Martinique, or in Madeira.

- **SINGLE BLENDED RUM**
  Single blended rum combines pot still and column still rums from a single distillery. They maintain consistency and a character that is unique to the distillery of origin.

TASTING
RUM

THE WORLD OF RUM TASTING is a rewarding journey of discovery. In this chapter, we'll take a trip through the art of rum appreciation, exploring every facet of the tasting experience. From crafting your own aroma kit to mastering the art of writing tasting notes, we'll uncover the secrets to unlocking rum's full potential. Learn how to use aroma descriptors to capture the essence of each rum, from the sweet scent of molasses and sugarcane honey to the spicy notes of oak and cinnamon. Discover the perfect glassware to enhance the tasting or drinking experience, and uncover the secrets to serving rums with flair. Whether you're a seasoned enthusiast or a curious newcomer, this chapter will empower you to savour every sip of rum with passion, precision, and poise.

MAKE YOUR OWN AROMA KIT

One of the most important tools when appreciating rum is the nose. Our sense of smell is closely linked to our sense of taste, and aroma contributes about 80 per cent of what we perceive as flavour. Here's a simple yet effective method to curate your personal cache of aromas to enhance your tasting sessions and deepen your understanding of rum.

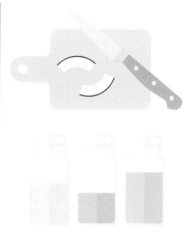

SELECT YOUR AROMAS

Start by identifying a range of aromas commonly found in rum. These can include fruity notes like banana, pineapple, or coconut; floral scents such as jasmine or hibiscus; grassy notes like fresh sugarcane or cut grass; spicy aromas like cinnamon, nutmeg, or cloves; and woody notes such as oak, cedar, or vanilla. You can also include other aromas like caramel, chocolate, coffee, honey, molasses, and citrus.

GATHER AROMATIC SOURCES

Once you've identified the aromas you want to include, gather aromatic sources to represent each one. This could include fresh or dried fruits like bananas and pineapple; dried spices like cinnamon sticks, cloves, and vanilla beans; woody aromas like cedar or oak chips; and other items like coffee beans, cocoa nibs, and fresh citrus peels.

PREPARE AND PACKAGE THE AROMAS

Prepare each item by cutting, crushing, or grinding it to release its scents and oils. Slice fresh fruits, crush spices with a mortar and pestle, or gently toast oak or cedar chips to enhance their aroma.

Package each aroma individually – small glass jars with airtight lids are ideal. Add neutral alcohol to preserve perishable sources, which will also help you to pick up the aroma mixed with alcohol.

ONCE YOU HAVE
ASSEMBLED YOUR
AROMA KIT, USE IT TO
ENHANCE YOUR RUM-
TASTING EXPERIENCES.

OPTIONAL EXTRAS

Depending on your preferences and budget, you may want to include additional items in your aroma kit, such as aroma strips or blotters for testing individual aromas, a flavour wheel (see pp100–01) or aroma guide to help identify different scents, or a notebook for recording your observations during tasting sessions (see "Writing tasting notes" on pp104–05).

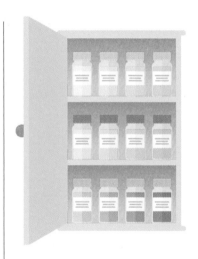

ORGANIZE YOUR KIT

Label each container clearly so you can easily identify the aromas during your tasting sessions. Arrange the packaged aromas in a box or tray in a logical order, such as grouping fruits or spices together, or organize them by intensity. Secure the containers well so that they won't spill or break during storage or transport.

STORE PROPERLY

Store your rum aroma kit in a cool, dry place away from direct sunlight to preserve the freshness and potency of the aromas – the back of a cupboard is ideal for this. Check the containers regularly for any signs of spoilage or deterioration, and replace any items as needed.

USE AND ENJOY

Once you have assembled your aroma kit, use it to enhance your rum-tasting experiences. Experiment by smelling different combinations of aromas to train your nose to recognize the aromas, and therefore flavours, found in rum. By training your senses, you will deepen your appreciation of the complex flavour profiles of this versatile spirit.

UNDERSTANDING FLAVOUR PROFILES

Understanding the intricacies of a rum profile can be daunting for many people. That aroma or flavour is sometimes just literally on the tip of your tongue.

RUM CHARACTERISTICS

Start by categorizing each rum according to broad flavour groups, such as sweet, spicy, or fruity. Then use aroma descriptors (see right) to help refine your evaluation.

SWEET

WOODY/OAKY

SWEET: Sweetness in rum can come from the natural sugars present in molasses or sugarcane juice. Naturally sweet rums, which are aged in oak wood, also get some sweetness from the wood sugars.

WOODY/OAKY: Rums that were aged in barrels, especially those that were previously used for ageing other alcohol, may develop woody flavours like oak, cedar, and sometimes a hint of smokiness.

SPICY

RICH

SPICY: Spicy characteristics can be derived naturally from the ageing process in wooden barrels or the addition of spices during production. Spicy notes include cinnamon, clove, and nutmeg.

RICH: Rich rums often have a full-bodied and complex flavour profile. They may include elements of chocolate, coffee, and even tobacco. Richness can come from both ageing and blending.

FRUITY

HERBAL/GRASSY

FRUITY: Fruity flavours in rum can range from tropical fruits, like pineapple, and orchard fruits, such as apple, to darker fruits, like raisins. Nuts, such as almonds, are also associated with fruity flavours.

HERBAL/GRASSY: Some rums exhibit herbal or grassy notes, especially those made from fresh sugarcane juice. They may have a lighter and more vegetal character, with hints of green herbs or fresh sugarcane.

RUM DESCRIPTORS

Here are a few descriptors to help you further evaluate
the aromas and flavours of the rum in your glass.

ALLSPICE
A spicy characteristic of
ground allspice and
sweet pimento.

ALMOND
An aromatic
associated with almond
or almond extract.

APPLE
An aromatic
characteristic of various
apple varieties.

APPLE/PEAR
A fruity-like aromatic
of pome fruits and not
a specific fruit.

ARTIFICIAL
Aromatics or tastes
considered artificial or
not natural for rum.

ASTRINGENT
An element that
smells or tastes
chemical.

BANANA
A fruity aromatic
characteristic of ripe
banana.

BITE
A burning sensation
felt on the tongue,
mouth, or throat.

BURNT
An element associated
with irritants to the
mucous membranes.

BUTTER
An aromatic
associated with
creamy butter.

BUTTERSCOTCH
A sweet aromatic
having both buttery
and caramelized notes.

CARAMEL
A term that describes
aromas/flavours of
chewy caramel.

CINNAMON
A sweet, woody
aromatic of ground
cinnamon bark.

PURE ETHANOL
A pungent aroma
associated with ethanol
(alcohol).

EUCALYPTUS/MINT
A sweet, green aroma
associated with fresh
mint or eucalyptus.

FLORAL
A fragrance
associated with
flowers.

FRUITY (GENERAL)
An aromatic associated
with non-specific fruits
including tropical.

FUSEL OIL
An aroma note
associated with isoamyl
alcohol and butanol.

LEATHERY
An aromatic
associated with
tanned animal hides.

MUSTY
An aromatic associated
with closed spaces: dry
(attic) or wet (cellar).

NUTTY
An aromatic
associated with
nuts or nut meats.

PETROL
A chemical solvent of
hydrocarbons, such as
petrol or kerosene.

PINEAPPLE
An aromatic
associated with
fresh pineapple.

SMOKE
A perception of
any kind of
smoke flavour.

SMOOTH
A clean, pleasant
element, especially
on the palate.

SPICY
An overall term
associated with
pungent spices.

SWEET
A taste stimulated by
sugars and other
sweeteners.

SYRUPY
An aroma associated
with viscous syrups like
maple syrup.

VANILLA
An aromatic blend
of sweet, vanillin,
and woody.

WOODY
An aromatic associated
with dry, freshly cut wood,
balsamic or bark-like.

RUM FLAVOUR WHEEL

A rum flavour wheel can help you visualize the relationship between certain rum aromas and flavours. The wheel is a great tool to use in conjunction with a rum aroma kit (see pp96–97).

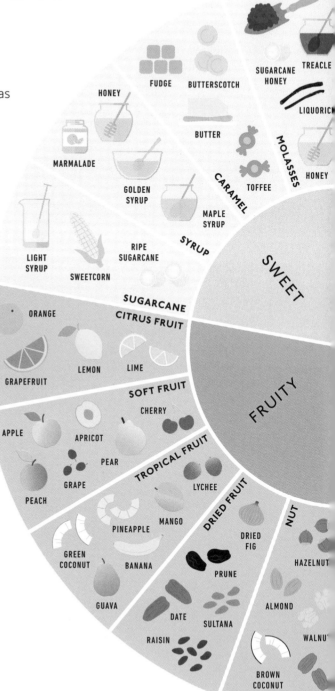

FRUITY FLAVOURS
Use the flavour wheel to identify what category of fruit you can taste

A WORLD OF FLAVOUR

Flavours in rum range from spicy, woody, and herbal to rich, fruity, and sweet. Once you have identified a broad category of aroma or flavour in your rum, use the flavour wheel to describe it in more detail.

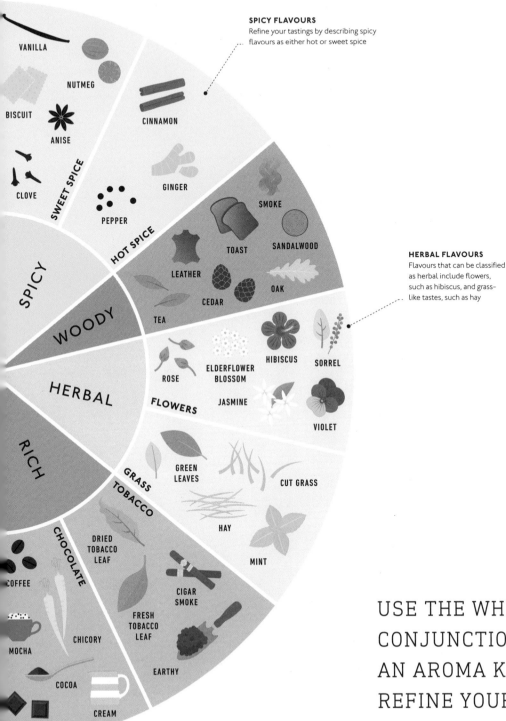

SPICY FLAVOURS
Refine your tastings by describing spicy flavours as either hot or sweet spice

HERBAL FLAVOURS
Flavours that can be classified as herbal include flowers, such as hibiscus, and grass-like tastes, such as hay

VANILLA

NUTMEG

BISCUIT

ANISE

CLOVE

SWEET SPICE

PEPPER

CINNAMON

GINGER

HOT SPICE

SMOKE

TOAST

SANDALWOOD

LEATHER

CEDAR

OAK

TEA

WOODY

SPICY

HERBAL

ROSE

ELDERFLOWER BLOSSOM

HIBISCUS

SORREL

JASMINE

FLOWERS

VIOLET

RICH

GRASS

TOBACCO

GREEN LEAVES

CUT GRASS

HAY

MINT

CHOCOLATE

DRIED TOBACCO LEAF

CIGAR SMOKE

COFFEE

FRESH TOBACCO LEAF

CHICORY

MOCHA

EARTHY

COCOA

CREAM

CHOCOLATE

USE THE WHEEL IN CONJUNCTION WITH AN AROMA KIT TO REFINE YOUR RUM-TASTING PALATE.

A SYSTEMATIC APPROACH TO TASTING RUM

Tasting rum can be an enjoyable and rewarding experience. But as there are hundreds of great rums on the market, waiting to caress your palate, how do you get the best out of the rum in your glass? Here's a six-step systematic approach you can follow to refine your rum tasting.

PREPARE YOUR TASTING ENVIRONMENT

Select a variety of rums to taste, such as a light rum from Cuba, a medium-bodied one from Venezuela, a heavy rum from Jamaica, a grassy, herbaceous rum from Martinique, and a spicy, savoury rum from Trinidad. Use clean, clear glasses and make sure you're in a well-lit and ventilated area, free from any strong odours that could interfere with your senses.

OBSERVE THE APPEARANCE

Pour a small amount of rum into your glass. Hold the glass up to the light and observe the colour and clarity of the rum. Note any differences between the rums you're evaluating. Some well-aged rums display the faintest tinge of jade at the rum's edges.

THE NOSE

Gently swirl the rum in the glass to release its aroma. Then, bring the glass to your nose and take a few short sniffs, breathing out through your mouth. Pay attention to the aromas you detect, such as fruity, floral, spicy, or woody notes. Use your homemade rum aroma kit as reference (see pp96–97).

TASTING RUM IS NOT JUST ABOUT
ANALYSING THE FLAVOURS – IT'S ALSO
ABOUT ENJOYING THE JOURNEY AND
THE STORIES BEHIND EACH BOTTLE.

THE PALATE

Take a small sip and let it coat your
mouth. Pay attention to the initial
flavours you perceive. Is it sweet,
dry, or somewhere in between?
Notice any specific flavours that
come through prominently. Take
another sip and let it linger on
your palate. Notice how the
flavours develop over time. Pay
attention to the texture (mouthfeel)
of the rum – is it smooth and creamy
or more sharp and astringent?

FINISH AND AFTERTASTE

Swallow the rum (or spit if you
wish) and pay attention to the
finish. Note any lingering flavours
or sensations that remain in your
mouth after you've swallowed.
Does the rum leave a warm,
spicy finish, or is it more subtle
and smooth? Is the finish long
or short?

TAKE NOTES

If you wish, jot down your
observations and impressions.
This will help you remember and
compare the different rums you've
tasted (see "Writing tasting notes"
on pp104–05). After tasting
several rums, take some time
to compare and contrast your
observations. Which rum did you
enjoy the most? What were the
key differences between them?

WRITING TASTING NOTES

Now armed with the essential tools to embark on your voyage through the diverse *terroirs* of rum, it's time to pen your tasting notes. Scribbling down your impressions can be fun and enlightening, as it immortalizes the intricate array of aromas, flavours, texture, and finish that define each rum.

WHAT'S THE STORY?

Begin by delving into the brand's backstory – its origins, distillation techniques, ageing regimen, and distinctive attributes. Consider the distillery's pedigree, the rum's price point, and any accolades it has garnered. With these insights in hand, embark on the journey of rum evaluation.

APPEARANCE

Use the steps outlined in "A systematic approach to tasting" on pp102–03 to guide you. Begin by observing the appearance of the rum. Note down the colour, clarity, and viscosity of the liquid. Describe the hue, which can range from pale straw to deep amber or mahogany, and any reflections or highlights you observe. Comment on the legs, or "tears", that form on the side of the glass when swirled – an indication of the rum's viscosity and alcoholic strength.

THE NOSE

Swirl the glass and sniff. Note the intensity and complexity of the aromas and describe the primary and secondary notes you detect. Look for fruity, sweet, spicy, woody, herbal, or rich aromas, as well as any nuances like caramel, vanilla, or chocolate. Consider the overall balance of the aromas.

THE PALATE

Take a small sip and note the initial flavours and their intensity. Refer to the rum descriptors and the flavour wheel on pp99–101 to help refine your observations.

Note down the sweetness, acidity, bitterness, or spiciness of the rum, as well as the mouthfeel.

Take another sip and notice how the flavours evolve and develop over time. Write down what you notice about the complexity and balance of the flavours, as well as any changes in intensity or character. Look for subtle transitions between different flavour profiles.

THE FINISH

Swallow or spit the rum and note any lingering flavours or sensations that remain in your mouth. Is the finish short and clean or long and lingering? What is your overall impression and satisfaction of the finish, such as any warmth, spice, or sweetness that persists?

YOUR RATING

Write down your overall rating of the rum. Reflect on its character, complexity, and quality, and any standout features. Compare the rum to others you've tasted. Also note any recommendations for the best way to drink the rum, whether neat, on the rocks, or in cocktails.

LOOK FOR FRUITY, SWEET, SPICY, WOODY, HERBAL, OR RICH AROMAS, AS WELL AS ANY NUANCES.

TASTING SHEET

Follow the guidelines opposite to write detailed and descriptive tasting notes that capture the essence of each rum and deepen your appreciation for this spirit.

RUM NAME ....

☐ NEAT   ☐ MIXER ....

APPEARANCE

....
....
....

RATING

☆ ☆ ☆ ☆ ☆

NOSE

AROMA INTENSITY

NEUTRAL   LIGHT   MEDIUM   STRONG

PALATE

FLAVOUR INTENSITY

NEUTRAL   LIGHT   MEDIUM   STRONG

SWEET

FRUITY   WOODY

RICH   HERBAL

SPICY

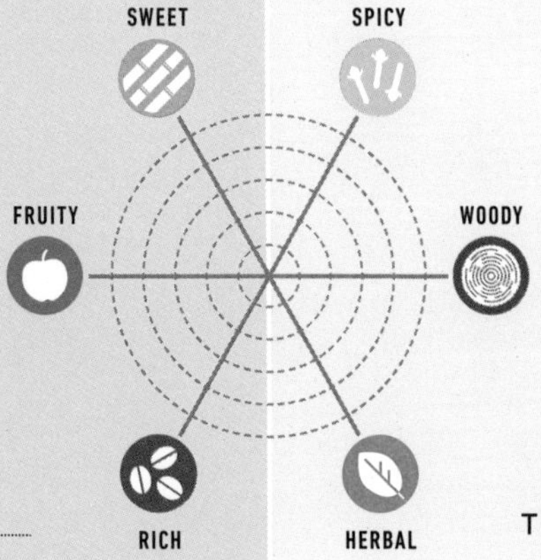

THE FINISH

DOES THE GLASS MATTER?

The choice of glassware can significantly impact the overall drinking experience when serving rum, whether neat, with a mixer, or in a cocktail. The right glass enhances the aroma, taste, and presentation of the rum, contributing to a more enjoyable and immersive experience.

THE RIGHT GLASS

Glassware not only influences the sensory experience but also contributes to the overall aesthetics of the drink. Additionally, the thickness and quality of the glass can affect the temperature of the rum. Choosing the right glass for the occasion and the specific type of rum being served can enhance the overall enjoyment of the spirit. That said, the most important glass is the one you're comfortable drinking from, but I wouldn't advise drinking a 30-year-old Jamaican rum from a pint glass.

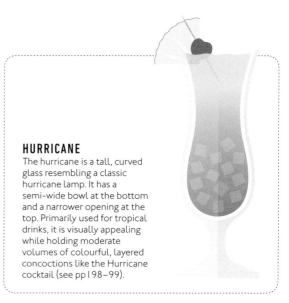

HURRICANE

The hurricane is a tall, curved glass resembling a classic hurricane lamp. It has a semi-wide bowl at the bottom and a narrower opening at the top. Primarily used for tropical drinks, it is visually appealing while holding moderate volumes of colourful, layered concoctions like the Hurricane cocktail (see pp198–99).

SNIFTER

With a wide bowl and narrow opening, snifter glasses are often preferred for aged and premium rums. The wide bowl allows for swirling, which can help release and concentrate the aromas, allowing you to appreciate the complex aromas and flavours of the spirit.

GLENCAIRN

Commonly used for whisky tasting, Glencairn glasses can also be suitable for rum tastings. Their shape concentrates the aromas, making them ideal for those who want to explore and appreciate the nuances of different rum varieties.

HIGHBALL OR COLLINS

Highball or Collins glasses are commonly used for mixed drinks and cocktails. They are suitable for long, refreshing, rum-based cocktails like a Cuba Libre, Dark 'n' Stormy, or Mojito (see pp192–93, 196–97, 206–07). The tall shape accommodates ice and mixers while showcasing the drink's colour.

STEMMED COCKTAIL

Coupe or martini glasses can be used for serving more elegant or upscale rum cocktails. Their wide opening allows cocktails to breathe and develop, like an unstrained Daiquiri (see pp194–95), as the chipped ice slowly dilutes on top of the refreshing drink.

ROCKS

Rocks glasses, also known as old fashioned or lowball glasses, are versatile and can be used for serving rum neat, on the rocks, or for short cocktails like the classic Old Fashioned. The wide opening allows for easy sipping and the addition of ice or water.

TROPICAL MUGS

Also known as tiki mugs, these vessels are often associated with tropical and exotic rum-based cocktails. The mug helps to conceal the drink, creating a sense of mystery as you sip. They also add a fun and quirky element, and are commonly used for drinks like a Mai Tai (see pp202–03).

POCO GRANDE

Also known as a *piña colada* glass, the *poco grande* has a wide bowl tapering slightly towards the top, often with a stem and footed base. It accommodates large volumes of cocktails, especially frozen drinks like a Piña Colada (see pp210–11). The spacious design also allows for ample ice and garnishes.

COPITA

These small, stemmed glasses with a tulip-shaped bowl are recommended for all styles of rums and are ideal for sampling different rums or conducting rum tastings. They concentrate the aromas and flavours, allowing you to evaluate the rum's characteristics in a controlled manner.

WAYS TO SERVE RUM

As a versatile base spirit, rum forms the foundation of countless cocktails, from timeless classics to modern creations. But as a spirit for all seasons and all occasions, there are many other ways to serve and enjoy this tropical tipple.

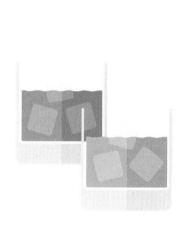

SERVE IT NEAT

Serving rum neat, or straight, is perhaps the purest way to enjoy the spirit. Simply pour the rum into a glass and sip it slowly, allowing the flavours to unfold on your palate. Neat rum allows you to fully appreciate the nuances of the spirit, from the natural aromas on the nose to the mouthful of flavour on your palate.

This method is perfectly suited for high-quality rums, particularly aged and superpremium varieties, which should be savoured like fine whisky or brandy.

ON THE ROCKS

When rum is served on the rocks – with ice – the ice helps to chill and dilute the liquid slightly, softening the flavours and creating a smoother drinking experience. On the rocks is a popular way to enjoy rum, particularly in warmer climates or as a refreshing aperitif.

Serving rum with ice is also a great way to showcase the complexity of aged rums, as the melting ice opens up new layers of flavour.

A SPLASH OF WATER

Adding a splash of water to rum can help release its aromas and flavours, making it more approachable and accessible, especially for those new to the spirit. The water helps to dilute the alcohol and soften the intensity of the rum, allowing you to better discern its nuances.

Adding water is particularly popular for drinking cask-strength high-proof rums or overproof varieties, as the water helps tame the heat and reveal hidden flavours. Also see pp110–11 for the best mixers to pair with rum.

PAIRING WITH FOOD

Rum pairs well with a wide range of foods,
from savoury dishes to sweet desserts.

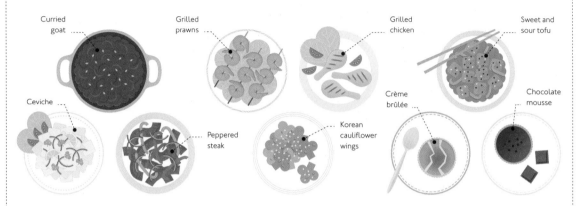

Curried goat

Grilled prawns

Grilled chicken

Sweet and sour tofu

Ceviche

Crème brûlée

Chocolate mousse

Peppered steak

Korean cauliflower wings

CARIBBEAN RUMS

Consider pairing rums from the
Caribbean with West Indian or Latin
American cuisine for an authentic and
flavourful dining experience that
celebrates the spirit's cultural heritage.

LIGHT AND FRUITY RUMS

Light and fruity rums are a natural
match for seafood, grilled meats, and
tropical-inspired dishes.

AGED AND HEAVY RUMS

Aged and heavy rums complement rich
and hearty food, like barbecued meat or
tofu, dark chocolate, and sweet desserts.

RUM AND CHOCOLATE

Rum and chocolate make for a
luxurious pairing, with the rich,
complex taste of the spirit
complementing the indulgent
sweetness of chocolate. Dark
chocolate, especially with a high
cocoa content, pairs particularly
well with aged rums, while milk
chocolate enhances the smoothness
of an unaged or lightly aged rum.

Dark chocolate pairs
particularly well
with aged rums

Milk chocolate
enhances the
smoothness of an
unaged or lightly
aged rum

FOR THE CIGAR LOVERS

If it grows together, it goes together,
which is why drinking rum with a cigar
is another popular way to serve a
premium rum that has been matured
in the tropics. After all, the island of
Cuba is known both for its rum *and*
its cigars. In the tropics, sugarcane
is grown in the same regions as
tobacco and tobacco-curing barns,
so it's entirely possible that the
tobacco leaves impart some of
their aroma to the sugarcane.

RUM HIGHBALLS

While sipping fine rum neat or on the rocks can be a delightful experience, it's not for everyone. Some prefer their rums as an ingredient in a long drink, so the addition of a mixer, especially when it's carbonated, opens up a spectrum of possibilities in the highball.

WHAT ARE HIGHBALLS?

A highball is a mixed alcoholic drink served in a highball glass, composed of an alcoholic base spirit and a larger proportion of a non-alcoholic mixer, often a carbonated beverage. Whether it's the sweetness of cola, the acidity of citrus soda, or the spice of ginger beer, fizzy mixers help to harmonize the different taste elements, ensuring that no single flavour dominates. This balance creates a more nuanced and enjoyable drinking experience for rum drinkers who just want a long, cool drink.

COLA

Classic cola pairs famously with rum in timeless cocktails such as a Rum and Coke or Cuba Libre (see pp192–93). The vanilla, caramel, and citrus combination of most colas naturally complements the rich flavours of rum, creating a simple yet satisfying drink. There are many flavoured colas, like vanilla, that marry well with a range of rums.

Cubre Libre

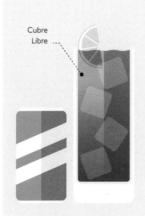

GINGER BEER

Ginger beer is a staple mixer for rum, particularly in cocktails like a Dark 'n' Stormy (see pp196–97) or a Rum Mule, which is made with rum, ginger beer, lime, and bitters. The bold, spicy flavour of ginger beer adds length and structure to the rum, resulting in a refreshing and invigorating beverage.

Dark 'n' Stormy

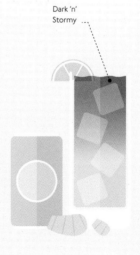

GINGER ALE

Slightly drier than most ginger beers, and lighter on the spiciness, ginger ale is nevertheless just as tasty with a light rum. Look for a variation such as spiced orange ginger ale to make an amazing Rum Buck cocktail of rum, ginger, and citrus.

Rum Buck

FIZZY MIXERS HELP TO HARMONIZE THE DIFFERENT TASTE ELEMENTS IN RUM, ENSURING THAT NO SINGLE FLAVOUR DOMINATES.

SODA WATER

Light and crisp soda water is a versatile mixer that pairs well with rum in drinks like a Rum Rickey (add a squeeze of lime). Its effervescence helps lighten up the drink while allowing the flavours of the rum to shine through, without being sweetened by any sugar.

Rum Rickey

TONIC WATER

Bitter tonic water adds a unique twist to rum drinks. The combination of tonic's bitterness with the sweetness of rum creates a sophisticated and refreshing drink. Try making a light rum and tonic with a twist of lemon, lime, or orange peel.

Light rum and tonic with a twist of citrus

CITRUS SODA

Citrus soda from brands such as Sprite or 7UP adds a sweet, citrussy kick to rum highballs. Its bright and tangy flavour pairs well with the sweetness of rum, resulting in a zesty and refreshing beverage. In the Caribbean and Australia, this type of mixer is jazzed up with a couple of dashes of bitters in a lemon, lime, and bitters (LLB), which goes well with rum.

Rum LLB

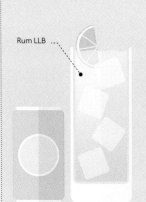

GRAPEFRUIT SODA

Tangy grapefruit soda adds a refreshing twist to many rum serves. In Jamaica, people often drink overproof rum with a sweet grapefruit soda called Ting. Its bright, citrus flavour pairs well with the sweetness of rum, creating a vibrant and lively beverage.

Grapefruit soda

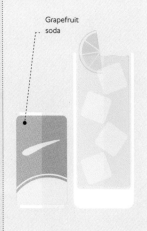

MAKING RUM COCKTAILS

Creating a balanced and flavourful cocktail with rum as
the key driver requires attention to detail, understanding
the characteristics of the rum, and a thoughtful
combination of complementary ingredients.

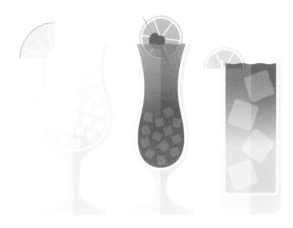

CHOOSE THE RIGHT RUM

Begin by selecting the right type of rum for your
cocktail. Rums vary widely in flavour, so consider
the cocktail you're making and choose a rum that
complements the other ingredients. Light rums
work well in citrussy drinks like a Daiquiri (see
pp194–95), while heavily aged rums add depth
to more complex cocktails like a Rum Manhattan.

THE FLAVOUR PROFILE

Consider the nuances of the
chosen rum's flavour profile.
Is it characterized by fruity notes,
hints of vanilla, or a pronounced
oakiness? This knowledge will
guide your choice of mixers,
garnishes, and other ingredients
to enhance and complement the
rum's inherent flavours.

CREATE A BALANCE

Aim for a balance between
sweetness and citrus elements
in your cocktail. Rum often has
a natural sweetness, so don't
overpower it with excessive sugary
ingredients. Freshly squeezed
citrus juices, like lime or orange,
can add brightness and acidity that
complement rum's sweetness.

EXPERIMENT WITH BITTERS

Bitters can be the secret weapon
in enhancing the complexity of a
rum-based cocktail. A few dashes
of aromatic or fruit-based bitters
can add depth, balance sweetness,
and elevate the overall drinking
experience. Experiment with
different types of bitters to find
the perfect match for your rum.

SYNERGIZE WITH SYRUPS

Explore syrups to add depth and unique flavours to your cocktail. Simple syrup is a staple (see p191), but consider infusing it with spices, herbs, or fruits. Cinnamon-infused syrup can enhance the spiciness in a dark rum, for instance, while a tropical fruit-infused syrup can amplify the flavours in a light rum.

USE FRESH INGREDIENTS

Whenever possible, use fresh and high-quality ingredients. Fresh herbs, fruits, and muddled ingredients can impart vibrant aromas and flavours that elevate the overall drinking experience. Garnish with citrus twists, mint sprigs, or fruit slices to add visual appeal and an extra layer of aroma.

EXPERIMENT WITH TEXTURE

Consider the mouthfeel, or texture, of your cocktail. Experiment with crushed ice, shaking techniques, or even incorporating creamy elements like coconut cream or egg whites for a velvety texture. Texture can enhance the overall drinking pleasure and make the cocktail more memorable.

CULTURAL INFLUENCES

Explore the cultural roots of the rum you're using. Different regions produce rums with unique characteristics (see "Navigating rum by region", pp114–87). Drawing inspiration from the traditional drinks of those regions can create a more authentic and rich cocktail experience.

TEMPERATURE MATTERS

Pay attention to serving temperatures. Some rum cocktails, such as the Treacle, benefit from being served over ice, while others, such as the Mary Pickford (see pp204–05), shine when served in a chilled glass. Experiment with temperature variations to find the ideal serving method for your specific cocktail.

PRESENTATION AND GARNISH

The visual appeal of a cocktail contributes significantly to the drinking experience. Garnish with ingredients that enhance the aroma and complement the flavours. A well-presented cocktail is not only enjoyable to drink but also a feast for the senses.

NAVIGATING
RUM
----- BY -----
REGION

NAVIGATING RUMS BY REGION is a fascinating way to explore the diverse flavour profiles, production methods, and cultural differences for some of the world's top rum. Each rum-producing country or region contributes unique characteristics shaped by its history and local regulations. Caribbean nations like Jamaica are renowned for bold, high-ester rums, while Cuba produces light-bodied and drier expressions. The French Caribbean produces *agricole* rums from sugarcane juice, offering grassy and vegetal notes. Spanish-speaking regions, such as the Dominican Republic, often produce light- or medium-bodied, sweeter rums. Central and South American countries craft rums that tend to lean towards a sweeter style of finish.

BARBADOS

To some, Barbados is the birthplace of rum, and it was here that the spirit was christened "rumbullion". It is also home to the world's oldest commercial rum distillery, founded in 1703.

WHAT MAKES BARBADIAN RUM UNIQUE?

Barbados follows the Caribbean Community (CARICOM) rum standards. These stipulate that Barbadian rum must be made from a sugarcane byproduct, cannot be bottled at less than 40% ABV, and that the age on the label can only refer to the youngest rum in the blend.

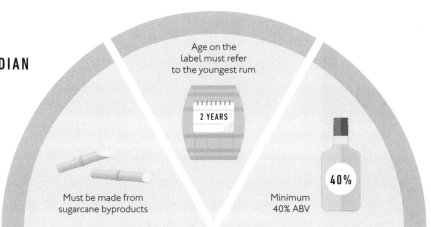

Age on the label must refer to the youngest rum

2 YEARS

Must be made from sugarcane byproducts

40%

Minimum 40% ABV

TYPES OF BARBADIAN RUM

The most popular rum brands on the island are younger ones, such as E.S.A. Field and Old Brigand, "the one-eyed man". Barbados is also home to the world's oldest rum distillery, Mount Gay, which makes several rums popular with tourists as the brand is sold in multiple countries around the world. Historically, there are brands like Stade's Rum from the West Indies Distillery or the St Nicholas Abbey rums, which are unique in that they are made from sugarcane syrup from their own estate sugarcane and 100 per cent pot stilled – most other Barbadian rums are blends of pot and column.

Barbados is now seen as one of the world leaders in superpremium aged rums. Both Mount Gay and Foursquare distilleries hold 90 per cent of the island's valuable aged stock, and they are leading the campaign to have Barbados rum recognized in the same way as superpremium Scotch, tequila, and Cognac.

MIXERS

FEVER-TREE Spiced Orange Ginger Ale

THE LONDON ESSENCE White Peach & Jasmine Crafted Soda

FRANKLIN & SONS Valencian Orange & Grapefruit

COCKTAILS

CORN 'N' OIL

DAIQUIRI see pp194–95

PIÑA COLADA see pp210–11

OTHER RUMS TO TRY

E.S.A. FIELD BARBADOS WHITE RUM

R.L. SEALE'S OLD BRIGAND BARBADOS RUM

STADE'S RUM BARBADOS BOND NO. 8

BAJAN 1966 GRAND RESERVE

40% ABV	MOLASSES	DOUBLE RETORT POT & COLUMN STILL	FOURSQUARE DISTILLERY

FLAVOUR

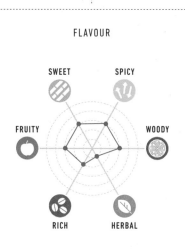

Bajan 1966 is named in honour of Barbados's independence, which it gained in 1966 after more than 300 years as a British colony.

This rum is distilled using a proprietary blend of column- and pot-still distillates, resulting in a complex, layered, and robust rum that tantalizes the palate. Aged in heavily charred American oak ex-bourbon barrels, the palate and aroma offer notes of caramel with a touch of vanilla, dried fruit, and a little pepper and spice.

DOORLY'S XO RUM

43% ABV	MOLASSES	DOUBLE RETORT POT & COLUMN STILL	FOURSQUARE DISTILLERY

FLAVOUR

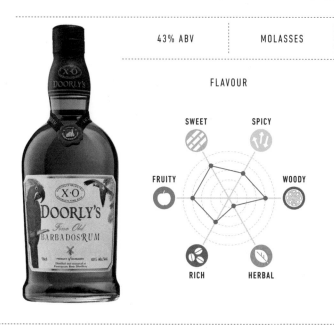

This blend of pot and column still rum is matured for at least six years in ex-bourbon barrels, with a further maturation in oloroso sherry casks. The XO on the label, meaning "extra old", indicates that the rum has been aged for at least six years.

This rum has a rich, fruity character of raisins and charred banana, with notes of toffee and vanilla throughout the palate, finishing with a buttery oak.

MOUNT GAY BLACK BARREL

| 43% ABV | MOLASSES | DOUBLE RETORT POT & COLUMN STILL | MOUNT GAY DISTILLERY |

FLAVOUR

SWEET · SPICY · WOODY · HERBAL · RICH · FRUITY

From the world's oldest working rum distillery (established in 1703), this is a blend of double retort pot and traditional column still rums. Matured in American oak for between three and seven years, they are finished in heavily charred ex-bourbon casks for six months before bottling.

Complex aromas of toasted oak, Caribbean spices, apples, and oranges fill the nose. The palate offers a balance of bold spices and juicy fruit, with hints of sweet caramel and creamy vanilla.

MOUNT GAY XO TRIPLE CASK BLEND

| 43% ABV | MOLASSES | DOUBLE RETORT POT & COLUMN STILL | MOUNT GAY DISTILLERY |

FLAVOUR

SWEET · SPICY · WOODY · HERBAL · RICH · FRUITY

Another great-tasting rum from the oldest working rum distillery in the world, and created by master blender Trudiann Branker, it is a marriage of double retort pot and traditional column still rums. After resting in a combination of American whiskey, bourbon, and Cognac casks, it's then blended and bottled at 43% ABV.

Aromas of vanilla, oak, and spice, with a taste of fruits, spices, and dark chocolate, culminate in a round, long finish of wood and salted caramel.

R.L. SEALE'S 10 YEAR OLD

46% ABV	MOLASSES	DOUBLE RETORT POT & COLUMN STILL	FOURSQUARE DISTILLERY

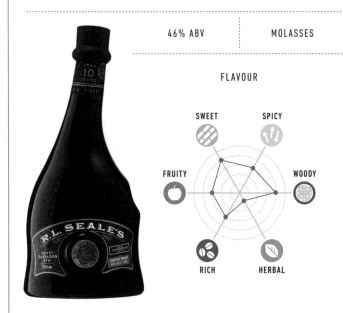

FLAVOUR

R.L. Seale & Co., founded in 1926 by Reginald Leon Seale, embraces the Barbados tradition of fine aged and blended rums. The Foursquare Distillery, which now makes this brand, is run by Richard Seale, Reginald's great-grandson.

The rum is a blend of double retort pot still and traditional column still that has been aged for a minimum of 10 years in ex-bourbon barrels. It has spicy, cooked apple notes with hints of vanilla, and naturally sweet, warm allspice, caramel, oak, and nuttiness on the palate.

ST NICHOLAS ABBEY 5 YEAR OLD

40% ABV	SUGARCANE SYRUP	HYBRID POT STILL	ST NICHOLAS ABBEY DISTILLERY

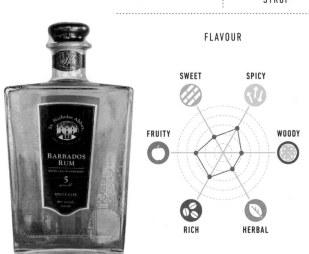

FLAVOUR

One of the oldest surviving sugar plantations in Barbados, St Nicholas Abbey great house was built in 1658, making it one of the few houses from the Jacobean era still standing in the western hemisphere.

The distillery, part of the estate, houses a specially designed pot still called Annabelle, which produces this light-bodied rum aged in ex-bourbon American oak barrels. It produces dry notes of vanilla, mocha coffee, and hazelnut, as well as fruity notes with white pepper.

JAMAICA

The Jamaican rum style is renowned for its strength, vigour, robust character, and a funkiness that has made it one of the most imitated styles of rum in the world.

WHAT MAKES JAMAICA RUM UNIQUE?

GI-compliant rums using the term "Jamaica Rum" on the label must be fermented and distilled in certain parts of the country. Pot or column stills with copper must be used, with small, wooden oak barrels to age and a minimum age claim. Sugar cannot be added.

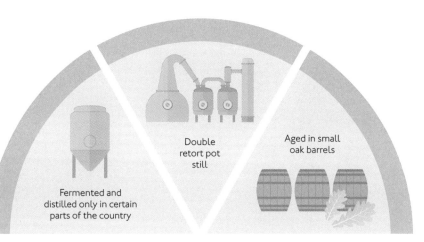

Fermented and distilled only in certain parts of the country

Double retort pot still

Aged in small oak barrels

TYPES OF JAMAICAN RUM

Jamaican rum often exhibits big, fruity, funky, and spicy notes owing to the island's unique fermentation and distillation techniques. The use of traditional double retort pot stills, dunder and muck pits (see pp88–89), and prolonged fermentation periods contribute to the complexity and depth of Jamaican rums. Overproofed rums at 63% ABV are the most popular style on the island.

Renowned brands like Appleton Estate and Hampden Estate also exemplify the quintessential Jamaican rum style, offering a diverse range of expressions from vibrant, white rums to full-bodied, aged varieties. Brands like Worthy Park use traditional triple distillation to create rich and flavoursome rums, perfect in cocktails such as a Piña Colada or Treacle. The Clarendon Distillery that makes Monymusk specializes in lighter-bodied rums that are great in a Mojito or served with ginger beer.

MIXERS	COCKTAILS	OTHER RUMS TO TRY
FEVER-TREE Spiced Orange Ginger Ale	**JUNGLE BIRD** see pp200–01	**CORUBA DARK**
OLD JAMAICA Ginger Beer	**MAI TAI** see pp202–03	**MYERS'S ORIGINAL DARK**
THE LONDON ESSENCE Roasted Pineapple Crafted Soda	**RUM PUNCH** see pp212–13	**BLACKWELL FINE JAMAICAN RUM**

APPLETON ESTATE 12 YEAR OLD RARE CASKS

| 43% ABV | MOLASSES | DOUBLE RETORT POT & COLUMN STILL | J. WRAY & NEPHEW |

FLAVOUR

SWEET   SPICY

FRUITY   WOODY

RICH   HERBAL

This rum is like a timeless piece of Jamaican art in a bottle. It's a versatile masterpiece that has been aged for a minimum of 12 tropical years in American white oak ex-bourbon casks.

With the heart of this luscious blend made in the Nassau Valley, you can expect a combination of rich molasses, oak, tropical fruit, and orange peel notes on the palate. The interaction with the barrel also introduces hints of vanilla, spice, and caramel.

HAMPDEN ESTATE 8 YEAR OLD

| 46% ABV | MOLASSES AND CANE JUICE | DOUBLE RETORT POT STILL | HAMPDEN ESTATE |

FLAVOUR

SWEET   SPICY

FRUITY   WOODY

RICH   HERBAL

When you think of Jamaica rum, it's usually rums from the north of the island that define the style. This eight-year-old rum, the flagship of the range, is produced with unique and semi-secret methods that have not changed since the 18th century. It's a perfect example of Hampden's aromatic complexity and versatility.

It has big, heavy, robust, and funky notes with tropical fruits and a long finish of sweet peppers and spice, making it a great all-rounder for sipping and mixing.

KINGSTON 62 GOLD

40% ABV	MOLASSES	DOUBLE RETORT POT & COLUMN STILL	J. WRAY & NEPHEW

FLAVOUR

SWEET · SPICY · WOODY · HERBAL · RICH · FRUITY

A rebrand of the former Appleton Special, this new label was released in 2020. The "62" refers to the year Jamaica gained independence from the United Kingdom. In Jamaica, rums like Kingston 62 Gold are affectionately known as "red rums".

Blended in traditional Jamaican style, this liquid gold is a fine, medium-bodied, lightly aged rum, made up of full-flavoured, traditional pot still and lighter-character, modern column still rums. The spicy and fruity notes of this rum work well with a mixer.

MONYMUSK CLASSIC GOLD 5 YEAR OLD

40% ABV	MOLASSES	DOUBLE RETORT POT & MULTI-COLUMN STILL	CLARENDON DISTILLERS LTD

FLAVOUR

SWEET · SPICY · WOODY · HERBAL · RICH · FRUITY

Monymusk Classic Gold is a blend of matured Jamaican rums crafted from the Long Pond Distillery in Trelawny, in the north of the island, and Clarendon Distillers, in the south.

The rum is aged in ex-bourbon barrels for a minimum of five years, and blended to create a profile with hints of ripe fruits, vanilla, and sweet caramel, making this a light but spicy rum. It can be enjoyed neat or in a cocktail, such as a Mojito (see pp206–07).

MONYMUSK SPECIAL RESERVE 10 YEAR OLD

40% ABV	MOLASSES	DOUBLE RETORT POT & MULTI-COLUMN STILL	CLARENDON DISTILLERS LTD

FLAVOUR

Being aged for a minimum of 10 tropical years in ex-bourbon barrels means that this rum has a lot of natural flavours, which have evolved through maturity.

A blend of pot still from Long Pond Distillery and column still from Clarendon, it is a tasty example of Jamaican rum blending, with aromas and flavours of sweet spice, tropical fruits, and light oak with a hint of coffee. The spicy oak finish, rich, silky feel, and fruitiness deliver a fullness of deep warmth and smoothness on the palate.

RUM-BAR GOLD

40% ABV	MOLASSES	DOUBLE RETORT POT STILL	WORTHY PARK ESTATE

FLAVOUR

With the rums made entirely from sugarcane grown on its own estate, Worthy Park brands, like Rum-Bar Gold, are true estate rums.

This rum is 100 per cent pot still and aged for a minimum of four years in ex–Jack Daniel's barrels, which bring the sweet aromas of ripe bananas and stewed apples. The fruit dominates on the palate, while the rum benefits from oak interaction, giving a vanilla and treacle-like sweetness. A long, mellow finish bursts with flavours.

RUM FIRE WHITE OVERPROOF

63% ABV	MOLASSES AND CANE JUICE	DOUBLE RETORT POT STILL	HAMPDEN ESTATE

FLAVOUR

The makers of Rum Fire developed it with the intention of crafting a white rum that remained loyal to the heavy pot-still style of Hampden Estate.

Thanks to the molasses (and a touch of cane juice vinegar) that go through extended fermentations with wild yeasts, the rum acquires the unique aromatic profile that Hampden Estate is famous for. It is powerful and funky, with an aromatic explosion of fruity taste, and aromas such as overripe banana, mango, pineapple, and spices.

WORTHY PARK 109

54.5% ABV	MOLASSES	DOUBLE RETORT POT STILL	WORTHY PARK ESTATE

FLAVOUR

This big and bold Jamaican rum is made in a copper pot still from estate-grown sugarcane molasses. It spends a short time in American oak and ex-bourbon casks, before being blended and bottled on site.

Exploding with tropical fruit notes, and classically bold Jamaican "funk", this full-strength dark rum is perfect for cocktails that require that extra oomph. Expect ripe banana and muscovado sugar, with a tropical essence of zesty pineapple, vanilla, and caramel.

WORTHY PARK SINGLE ESTATE RESERVE

45% ABV	MOLASSES	DOUBLE RETORT POT STILL	WORTHY PARK ESTATE

FLAVOUR

SWEET · SPICY · WOODY · HERBAL · RICH · FRUITY

Crafted in a double retort copper pot still, and made from estate-grown sugarcane molasses, this classic Jamaican rum was the first release under the Worthy Park range of bottlings. Aged between six and 10 years in American oak, it is matured, blended, and bottled entirely on site.

The punchy aromas of light tobacco, oak, spicy raisins, and plums complement the taste of tropical fruit, buttery soft wood, and a hint of pepper and ginger on the finish.

WRAY & NEPHEW WHITE OVERPROOF RUM

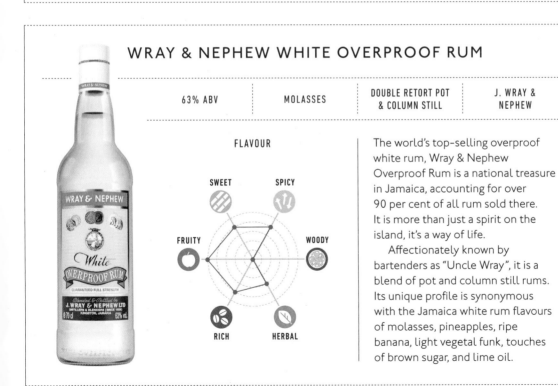

63% ABV	MOLASSES	DOUBLE RETORT POT & COLUMN STILL	J. WRAY & NEPHEW

FLAVOUR

SWEET · SPICY · WOODY · HERBAL · RICH · FRUITY

The world's top-selling overproof white rum, Wray & Nephew Overproof Rum is a national treasure in Jamaica, accounting for over 90 per cent of all rum sold there. It is more than just a spirit on the island, it's a way of life.

Affectionately known by bartenders as "Uncle Wray", it is a blend of pot and column still rums. Its unique profile is synonymous with the Jamaica white rum flavours of molasses, pineapples, ripe banana, light vegetal funk, touches of brown sugar, and lime oil.

MARTINIQUE

In recent times, the spirit of Martinique has been the flag bearer globally for rums made from fresh sugarcane juice, as well as rums that are protected by an *appellation d'origine contrôlée* (AOC).

WHAT MAKES MARTINICAN RUM UNIQUE?

Martinican *rhum agricole*, with its rich, volcanic *terroir*, adheres strictly to the AOC designation. The *rhum* must be exclusively produced from local, freshly pressed sugarcane juice, and must be distilled in a single column at between 65% and 75% ABV.

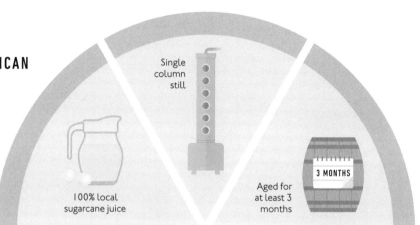

Single column still

100% local sugarcane juice

Aged for at least 3 months

3 MONTHS

TYPES OF MARTINICAN RUM

When sampling Martinican *rhums*, begin with *rhum blanc*, prized for its grassy notes and versatility in cocktails. For a richer experience, delve into aged varieties, such as *réserve spéciale* or VSOP, aged in oak barrels for at least four years and perfect for sipping neat or in cocktails. Embrace the island's heritage with *hors d'âge* or XO, aged for a minimum of six years and boasting refined flavours of caramel, spice, and tropical fruit.

- **Rhum blanc:** unaged rum that has been laid still for at least three months, and not more than three months if the rum has been stored in oak barrels.

- **Élevé sous bois:** aged for at least one year in oak casks.
- **Vieux:** aged for at least three years.
- **Très vieux, réserve spéciale, cuvée spéciale, VSOP:** aged for at least four years.
- **Extra vieux, grande réserve, hors d'âge, XO:** aged for at least six years.

MIXERS

TING Sparkling Grapefruit

THE LONDON ESSENCE Roasted Pineapple Crafted Soda

THREE CENTS Pink Grapefruit Soda

COCKTAILS

DAIQUIRI see pp194–95

MAI TAI see pp203–04

TI PUNCH see pp214–15

OTHER RUMS TO TRY

DILLON XO

J. BALLY 12 YEAR OLD

MAISON LA MAUNY XO

A1710 LA PERLE RARE RED CANE VINTAGE 2023

54.2% ABV	SUGARCANE JUICE	COPPER POT & CREOLE COLUMN STILL	A1710, HABITATION DU SIMON

FLAVOUR

SWEET · SPICY · FRUITY · WOODY · RICH · HERBAL

Boasting two Charentais copper pot stills with Creole columns, A1710 is a unique distillery on Martinique. The A1710 *rhums* do not comply with the French rules governing Martinique *rhum agricole* so cannot be classed as AOC Martinique Rhum Agricole.

The juice from a local sugarcane variety, red cane, is fermented for five days and distilled in batches, creating a rum with a floral aroma of rose and notes of pomegranate, with a delicate, natural sweetness of ripened sugarcane.

RHUM CLÉMENT 10 YEAR OLD

42% ABV	SUGARCANE JUICE	CREOLE COLUMN STILL	HABITATION CLÉMENT

FLAVOUR

SWEET · SPICY · FRUITY · WOODY · RICH · HERBAL

Habitation Clément is said to be the birthplace of *rhum agricole*. Every year, it releases carefully selected aged *rhums agricoles* as part of its Grande Réserve portfolio.

Distilled at Fonds-Préville Distillery in the north of the island, Rhum Clément 10 Year Old is matured in a combination of virgin and re-charred oak barrels, yielding characteristics of cinnamon, vanilla, toffee, cherries, almonds, and dried fruit, with a light, oaky finish.

DEPAZ PORT CASK FINISH

45% ABV	SUGARCANE JUICE	CREOLE COLUMN STILL	DEPAZ DISTILLERY

FLAVOUR

The Depaz Distillery, founded in 1917, is located near the town of Saint-Pierre, which was once the largest rum port in the world. The distillery still operates today thanks to an old steam engine. The rhum, matured for at least eight years in specially selected small oak casks, is finished for 11 months in old port casks.

It has light oak notes with aromas of vanilla and ripe fruits. On the palate, there are flavours of dried fruit, cocoa, jasmine, and coffee, with a mature port and tannic finish.

HBS SÉLECTION VARIÉTALE CANNE BLEUE 55

55% ABV	SUGARCANE JUICE	CHARENTAIS COPPER POT STILL	HBS L'HABITATION BEAUSÉJOUR

FLAVOUR

L'Habitation Beauséjour makes rhum outside the controlled appellation of the AOC Martinique. For HBS rhum agricole, the distillery uses cane from its own land.

Red and blue cane are the main varieties used, and the latter was chosen for the Sélection Variétale because of its exceptional sugar content. The fermented cane juice is distilled in a Charentais still topped by a column. The rum has a profile of fresh sugarcane, ripe banana, and floral notes.

HSE BLACK SHERIFF AMERICAN BARREL

| 40% ABV | SUGARCANE JUICE | CREOLE COLUMN STILL | HABITATION SAINT-ETIENNE |

FLAVOUR

SWEET · SPICY · WOODY · HERBAL · RICH · FRUITY

Black Sheriff asserts its character from the Kentucky bourbon barrels that it is matured in. Although the *rhum* is distilled at the Simon Distillery, the distillate is matured in the cellars of the Habitation Saint-Etienne.

The ex-bourbon barrels naturally give notes of vanilla and stone fruit with oak and smoky notes to this blend of three- to four-year-old *rhums*. The palate brings fruity notes with a medium to long finish of spices and wood.

LA FAVORITE COEUR DE CANNE 2 YEARS

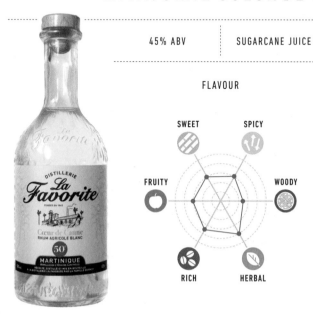

| 45% ABV | SUGARCANE JUICE | CREOLE COLUMN STILL | LA FAVORITE DISTILLERY |

FLAVOUR

SWEET · SPICY · WOODY · HERBAL · RICH · FRUITY

One of the last independent distilleries in Martinique, La Favorite was founded in 1842 on the remains of a sugar refinery called Les Jambettes, before being renamed La Favorite in 1851.

Coeur de Canne 2 Years is aged in casks for a minimum of two years. This ageing helps to combine the freshness and grassiness of the local cane distillate with the deliciously honeyed, floral, fruity, flambéed banana and vanilla notes we expect from the transformation in oak barrels.

NEISSON RHUM BLANC 52.5

52.5% ABV	SUGARCANE JUICE	SINGLE COLUMN SAVALLE STILL	NEISSON DISTILLERY

FLAVOUR

SWEET · SPICY · WOODY · HERBAL · RICH · FRUITY

Neisson *rhum* is produced at the family-owned distillery by master distiller Grégory Vernant Neisson and his mother, Claudine. Neisson is known for using non-hybrid varieties of sugarcane in its rums, like Malanoi, Rubanée, and Cristalline.

The sugarcane juice used to make *rhum agricole* has a considerable impact on the flavour of this spirit. It has a silky texture, with complex notes of freshly cut grass, cane juice, and tropical fruit, with floral aromas.

RHUM J.M XO

45% ABV	SUGARCANE JUICE	CREOLE COLUMN STILL	FONDS-PRÉVILLE DISTILLERY

FLAVOUR

SWEET · SPICY · WOODY · HERBAL · RICH · FRUITY

The Rhum J.M Distillery is located in the foothills of the active volcano Mount Pelée in the north of the island. All the sugarcane juice used to make its *rhums* is sourced from the surrounding estate, with the juice being pressed within an hour of harvest.

The XO is aged for six years in ex-bourbon barrels, creating a beautiful copper tone and complex flavour profile that is floral with dried fruits and jams, turning into a rich honey, spice, and almond on the palate.

SAINT JAMES XO

43% ABV	SUGARCANE JUICE	CREOLE COLUMN STILL	SAINT JAMES DISTILLERY

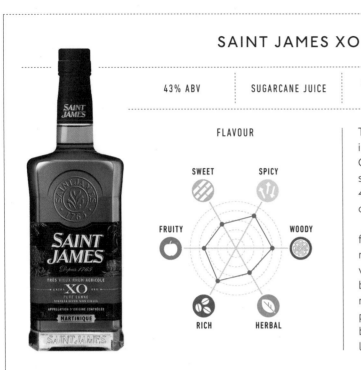

FLAVOUR

SWEET · SPICY · WOODY · HERBAL · RICH · FRUITY

The Saint James brand, founded in 1765, is one of the oldest in the Caribbean. Its six Creole column stills (and a pot still) produce over 4 million litres (880,000 gallons) of rum per year.

The XO, a blend of rums aged from six to 10 years, has a beautiful richness and depth, with aromas of vanilla and caramel and hints of cigar box. A good length is supported by roasted notes of mocha, and coffee, prunes, and figs on a delicately spicy background, with a touch of liquorice and black pepper.

TROIS RIVIÈRES DOUBLE WOOD AMBRÉ

43% ABV	SUGARCANE JUICE	CREOLE COLUMN STILL	RIVIÈRE-PILOTE, LA MAUNY ESTATE

FLAVOUR

SWEET · SPICY · WOODY · HERBAL · RICH · FRUITY

Distilled and matured at Rivière-Pilote in the south of Martinique, Trois Rivières Double Wood acquires its structure and flavour profile from the double ageing technique. This *rhum ambré* (amber rum) is matured for seven months in large American oak vats, followed by nine months in small French oak ex-whisky casks.

Rich aromas of dried fruit, stewed fruit, honey, coffee, and toasted oak fill the nose, complemented by notes of walnut oil, baking spices, black pepper, brown sugar, cocoa, and dried fruit throughout the palate.

GUADELOUPE

Guadeloupe, an archipelago in the Caribbean, is renowned for producing rums of a variety of styles that encapsulate the French-Caribbean spirit. It is divided into three main regions – Grande-Terre, Basse-Terre, and Marie-Galante.

WHAT MAKES GUADELOUPEAN RUM UNIQUE?

To use the protected designation "Rhum de Guadeloupe", the growing and processing of sugarcane, distillation, ageing, and bottling must occur within the geographical area of Guadeloupe. *Rhums* from Marie-Galante can add that designation to their name.

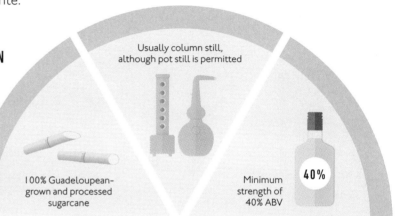

100% Guadeloupean-grown and processed sugarcane

Usually column still, although pot still is permitted

Minimum strength of 40% ABV

40%

TYPES OF GUADELOUPEAN RUM

The islands are home to several *rhum agricole* distilleries, which use freshly pressed sugarcane juice and traditional column stills to make their *rhums*. These present a spectrum of flavours, from grassy and herbal notes to hints of tropical fruit and spices. The vibrant character makes them ideal for sipping neat or elevating classic cocktails like the Ti Punch. The tropical notes in Guadeloupean rums also complement citrus-based cocktails like the Daiquiri or the classic Rum Sour. On the island of Marie-Galante, a classic Rum Punch is made with local *rhums* such as Rhum Bielle 3 Years and Bellevue VSOP. Whether you're exploring the earthy richness of Damoiseau *rhums* or the aromatic allure of Papa Rouyo *rhums*, Guadeloupean *rhums* offer a captivating journey through the flavours of the French Caribbean, making them a must-try for rum enthusiasts and cocktail connoisseurs alike.

MIXERS

TING Sparkling Grapefruit
THE LONDON ESSENCE Roasted Pineapple Crafted Soda
THREE CENTS Pink Grapefruit Soda

COCKTAILS

DAIQUIRI see pp194–95
MAI TAI see pp202–03
TI PUNCH see pp214–15

OTHER RUMS TO TRY

MARIE-LOUISE RHUM BLANC
RHUM RHUM PMG (41%)
SÉVERIN VSOP RHUM
VIEUX AGRICOLE 42°

HABITATION BELLEVUE VSOP 4 YEAR OLD

| 45% ABV | SUGARCANE JUICE AND MOLASSES | CREOLE COLUMN STILL | HABITATION BELLEVUE |

FLAVOUR

SWEET · SPICY · FRUITY · WOODY · RICH · HERBAL

Founded in 2001, Bellevue is the Caribbean's first eco-positive distillery. It is 100 per cent non-polluting and is recognized as the most modern unit in the French West Indies.

The four-year-old VSOP is a rare blend of *agricole* and traditional rum. Complex and varied, it highlights woody aromas, caramel, vanilla, fruit, spices, and hints of liquorice, as well as notes of tobacco, with a woody, spicy, and smoky finish.

RHUM BIELLE 3 YEARS

| 41% ABV | SUGARCANE JUICE | CREOLE COLUMN STILL | BIELLE DISTILLERY |

FLAVOUR

SWEET · SPICY · FRUITY · WOODY · RICH · HERBAL

Bielle was founded at the end of the 19th century and today is run by Dominique Thiery, who has built a reputation for Bielle as the island's top producer.

This pure cane juice rum is the signature of the Bielle house: slow fermentation, distillation in a Creole column, then ageing in ex-bourbon barrels. Vanilla, wood, fruits, sugarcane, floral, and vegetal aromas mingle with gingerbread, sweet jam, wood, honey, and a touch of pepper on the palate.

RHUM BOLOGNE VSOP

| 42% ABV | SUGARCANE JUICE | COPPER COLUMN STILL | BOLOGNE DISTILLERY |

FLAVOUR

SWEET · SPICY · FRUITY · WOODY · RICH · HERBAL

The Bologne Distillery, the oldest in Guadeloupe, is located on a 300-year-old cane plantation that stretches from the slopes of the Grande Soufrière volcano to the Caribbean Sea.

The rum is distilled to around 55–60% ABV, allowing more of the natural cane flavour to be present. It is then aged in French oak barrels for a minimum of eight years. The final blend gives notes of candied fruits, cinnamon, and iodine, with vanilla, star anise, and banana on the palate.

DAMOISEAU CONCORDIA

| 40% ABV | SUGARCANE JUICE & MOLASSES | COLUMN STILL | DAMOISEAU DISTILLERY |

FLAVOUR

SWEET · SPICY · FRUITY · WOODY · RICH · HERBAL

Damoiseau Distillery – originally known as the Bellevue au Moule Distillery – was established in the 19th century by the Rimbaud family of Martinique.

Concordia, "harmony" in Latin, is a blend of 60 per cent agricultural rum and 40 per cent traditional rums from Guadeloupe, both aged for a minimum of four years in small American barrels. It has light citrus, dried fruit, fresh cane, and light, woody aromas with peppers, cinnamon, sandalwood, and more fruit on the palate.

KARUKERA BLACK EDITION ALLIGATOR

45% ABV	SUGARCANE JUICE	COLUMN STILL	RHUMERIE KARUKERA

FLAVOUR

SWEET · SPICY · FRUITY · WOODY · RICH · HERBAL

Distilled at the Espérance Distillery, also known as the Longueteau Distillery, this rum is blended and aged at the nearby Rhumerie Karukera. After four years of ageing in French oak barrels, it is finished in new casks that have an alligator char (see p81).

Charring allows the liquid to interact more with the uncharred oak, giving brown sugar notes and intense smoky and spicy aromas. The palate has flavours of dried fruit, clove, nutmeg, and almond. The finish is long lasting and sweet.

LONGUETEAU PRÉLUDE

50.3% ABV	SUGARCANE JUICE	COLUMN STILL	ESPÉRANCE DISTILLERY

FLAVOUR

SWEET · SPICY · FRUITY · WOODY · RICH · HERBAL

Distilled at the Espérance Distillery, also known as the Longueteau Distillery, Prélude is the latest edition of the Longueteau rum series in the Harmonie collection.

Bottled at cask strength, the liquid is distilled from both red and blue cane varieties. The barrels are French oak with a light toasting, creating big floral and fruity aromas of sugarcane with a light, zesty aroma. The palate is sweet, caramelized oak with touches of peppers and spice.

MONTEBELLO RHUM VIEUX AGRICOLE 6 YEARS

42% ABV	SUGARCANE JUICE	TWO-COLUMN COPPER STILL	CARRÈRE DISTILLERY

FLAVOUR

SWEET · SPICY · FRUITY · WOODY · RICH · HERBAL

More commonly referred to as Montebello after its flagship rum brand, the Carrère Distillery operates a two-column copper still, which it uses to make several rum brands.

This Montebello rum has been aged for six years in American oak ex-bourbon and Cognac barrels. Its softness and fragrance give it a unique character of exotic fruits, candied citrus, and berries on the nose, with a medium-bodied mouthfeel of mango, caramel, vanilla, oak, and cooked fruits.

PAPA ROUYO ESB SANBLAJ POT STILL 2022

48.5% ABV	SUGARCANE JUICE	POT STILL	PAPA ROUYO DISTILLERY

FLAVOUR

SWEET · SPICY · FRUITY · WOODY · RICH · HERBAL

This pot still, double-distilled rum is made from Papa Rouyo's own sugarcane, grown in its Le Moule cane field. Meaning "blend" in Creole, Sanblaj is made from different barrels of this rum, aged in cellars for about a year.

A combination of new French barrels with intense charring, new American barrels with intermediate charring, and ex-Cognac red barrels creates the character of light berries, citrus peel, tannins, light spices, dried fruit, and menthol.

PÈRE LABAT XO 42°

42% ABV	SUGARCANE JUICE	CREOLE COLUMN STILL	POISSON DISTILLERY

FLAVOUR

SWEET · SPICY · WOODY · HERBAL · RICH · FRUITY

Poisson Distillery, also known as Père Labat Distillery, is the oldest on Marie-Galante. The estate has distilled rum since the early 1900s and still uses only locally grown sugarcane varieties.

The XO is aged for a minimum of six years in ex-bourbon American oak casks. This gives sweet, candied fruits with a hint of smoke and spice on the nose. On the palate, there is a little sugarcane and herbs like sage and tarragon, with light oak and peppers.

REIMONENQ JR CUVÉE SPÉCIALE

40% ABV	SUGARCANE JUICE	DOUBLE STAINLESS STEEL COLUMN	REIMONENQ DISTILLERY

FLAVOUR

SWEET · SPICY · WOODY · HERBAL · RICH · FRUITY

The Reimonenq Distillery was established in 1916. Its JR Cuvée Spéciale rum is distilled in a unique double stainless steel column, then aged for three years in ex-bourbon barrels that are stored in old cellars to control the tropical ageing.

It has aromas of light oak, nuts, and a touch of butter. In the mouth, it reveals pleasant woody flavours enhanced with spicy notes and dried apricot, with a dry finish of liquorice and pepper.

CUBA

Without doubt, rums made in Cuba have historically been an inspiration and influence to rum makers worldwide, as they sought to create lighter rums through distillation and ageing techniques the Cuban way.

WHAT MAKES CUBAN RUM UNIQUE?

There are strict guidelines for what defines a Cuban rum: it must use 100 per cent Cuban sugarcane and molasses, be distilled by column still only, age for a minimum of two years in American oak, and have a maximum bottle strength of 45% ABV.

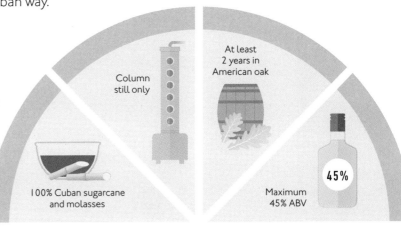

100% Cuban sugarcane and molasses

Column still only

At least 2 years in American oak

Maximum 45% ABV

45%

TYPES OF CUBAN RUM

Which Cuban rum should you stock on your bar? Just as Scotland has whisky made in different parts of the country, which influences the flavour, the nuances of different Cuban rums are reflected by the regional profile of the *terroir* where they are created.

Rums from west Cuba are known for being intense, dry, and punchy, like Havana Club 7 Años – perfect for classic Cuban cocktails such as El Presidente.

Rums from the east are known for their subtle smoothness and fruity aromas, like Santiago de Cuba 11, and are ideal for drinking neat or with a cube of ice.

Rums from the centre of the island, like Eminente Reserva 7 (Villa Clara province) and Ron la Progresiva 13 (Ciego de Avila province), are known for their light, fruity aromas, spices, and natural sweetness, and are perfect for cocktails such as a Daiquiri and Rum Sour. So, why not stock one from each region of Cuba?

MIXERS

SEKFORDE Lime, Mint, & Cacao Soda

LUSCOMBE Sicilian Lemonade

FEVER-TREE Madagascan Cola

COCKTAILS

CUBA LIBRE see pp192–93

DAIQUIRI see pp194–95

MOJITO see pp206–07

OTHER RUMS TO TRY

RON SANTERO 11 AÑOS

RON VARADERO AÑEJO

RON CANEY AÑEJO CENTURIA

EMINENTE RESERVA 7 AÑOS

41.3% ABV	MOLASSES	MULTI-COLUMN STILL	CORPORACIÓN CUBA RON SA

FLAVOUR

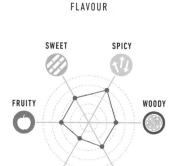

SWEET · SPICY · WOODY · HERBAL · RICH · FRUITY

A testament to Cuban craftsmanship, this rum unfolds on the palate like a rich tapestry of Cuban rum history. Made with 100 per cent Cuban sugarcane, it takes advantage of a high percentage of what the Cuba rum masters call *aguardiente*, which is similar to a molasses *eau de vie*.

The seven years in barrel deliver a very complex profile, with vibrant fruit and hints of dry cherry and spice, giving way to waves of chocolate, coffee, and tobacco.

HAVANA CLUB AÑEJO 7 AÑOS

40% ABV	MOLASSES	MULTI-COLUMN STILL	HAVANA CLUB DISTILLERY

FLAVOUR

SWEET · SPICY · WOODY · HERBAL · RICH · FRUITY

Wonderfully flavoursome, this Cuban rum has become iconic in recent times. When it was first created, it was the first Havana Club expression that was intended for sipping neat rather than for using in cocktails and mixed drinks.

It has aromas of sweet, buttery toffee, honeycomb, and coffee, a little spice, and dried citrus peels, with green orchard fruits and biscuits. The full, rich palate has notes of cigar box, cedarwood, guava, and banana leaf, with more toffee on the end.

LA PROGRESIVA DE VIGIA MEZCLA 13

41% ABV	MOLASSES	MULTI-COLUMN STILL	ENRIQUE VARONA DISTILLERY

FLAVOUR

SWEET · SPICY · WOODY · HERBAL · RICH · FRUITY

One of the oldest Cuban brands, Vigia is distilled at the Enrique Varona Distillery and named after Ernest Hemingway's island retreat.

This dry, premium rum was created by a team of master blenders from rum casks aged between 11 and 15 years old. Mezcla 13 ("Blend 13") was the 13th cask combination the blenders tried in the search for the right balance. It oozes notes of pear, prunes, and dried citrus zests, with light oak, cayenne pepper, and dark chocolate.

RON CUBAY RESERVA ESPECIAL 10

40% ABV	MOLASSES	MULTI-COLUMN STILL	LA RONERA CENTRAL

FLAVOUR

SWEET · SPICY · WOODY · HERBAL · RICH · FRUITY

Known locally as the "Pearl of the Cuban rums", Ron Cubay was first produced in 1964 in Santo Domingo after the Cuban revolution. It is now produced with a few other brands at La Ronera Central.

Like most aged Cuban rums, this rum is aged in ex-whisky barrels. This ageing creates aromas of honey, stone fruit, brown sugar, and vanilla, with a palate of toffee fudge, oak spices, and more vanilla.

SANTIAGO DE CUBA RON EXTRA AÑEJO 11

40% ABV	MOLASSES	MULTI-COLUMN STILL	CORPORACIÓN CUBA RON

FLAVOUR

This Santiago de Cuba is produced in the city of the same name, known for its rich history in rum production. Crafted with precision and aged to perfection, it emanates the soulful essence of Cuba.

It is a rum with rhythm and soul that dances on your tongue with the rich, tropical flavours of the sugarcane molasses. The palate offers notes of cinnamon, green banana, black pepper, caramel, vanilla, grilled pineapple, and coconut, which linger on the finish.

SAOCAN RESERVA ORIGINAL 10

40% ABV	MOLASSES	MULTI-COLUMN STILL	RONERA CÁRDENAS

FLAVOUR

Since 1878, SaoCan has been rooted in the Cuban tradition, when Spanish industrialist José Arechabala began the first production of *aguardiente* and rum in Cárdenas. It takes its name "SaoCan" from a fusion of "Saoco" and "Canchánchara", two of the oldest-known Cuban cocktails.

Blended then aged for 10 years in oak casks, this is a classic Cuban rum. It offers intense flavours of oaky vanilla, butterscotch, candied fruits, and baking spices throughout the palate.

PUERTO RICO

Renowned for their light and subtle character, Puerto Rican rums are some of the most consumed spirits, not only in the Caribbean but all over the world.

WHAT MAKES PUERTO RICAN RUM UNIQUE?

According to the Puerto Rico Industrial Development Company, all Puerto Rican rum must be made on the island with continuous distillation and aged in white oak barrels for at least a year. Gold rums are aged for at least two years, and premium rums at least six years.

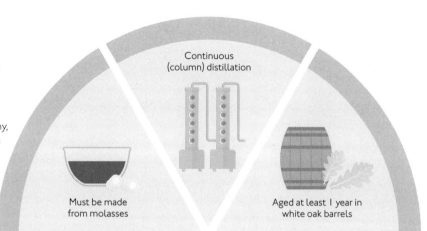

Continuous (column) distillation

Must be made from molasses

Aged at least 1 year in white oak barrels

TYPES OF PUERTO RICAN RUM

A small island in the north of the Caribbean, Puerto Rico is one of the biggest exporters of rum in the world. Leading the charge is the BACARDÍ brand, which has been made in Puerto Rico since 1936. Rums like the BACARDÍ Superior and the BACARDÍ Gran Reserva Diez have proved not only to be great additions to popular cocktails such as the Daiquiri and the Cuba Libre, but also craft cocktails such as the Mary Pickford benefit from these light-bodied rums.

On the island, there are two brands that many resident Puerto Ricans call for. The first is Don Q, from Ponce in the south of the island. It's a lightly aged rum and its versatility lends itself to cocktails like the Piña Colada and the Mojito. The other is Ron del Barrilito, from Bayamón, near the capital, San Juan. This small batch, golden craft rum can be enjoyed neat, on the rocks, with a mixer, or in cocktails such as an Old Fashioned or El Presidente.

MIXERS	COCKTAILS	OTHER RUMS TO TRY
FEVER-TREE Mexican Lime Soda **THREE CENTS** Pineapple Soda **FRANKLIN & SONS** Pressed Raspberry Lemonade	**DAIQUIRI** see pp194–95 **MOJITO** see pp206–07 **PIÑA COLADA** see pp210–11	**RON DEL BARRILITO 3 STARS** **PALO VIEJO GOLD** **TRIGO RESERVA AÑEJA**

BACARDÍ GRAN RESERVA DIEZ

40% ABV	MOLASSES	MULTI-COLUMN STILL	BACARDI DISTILLERY

FLAVOUR

Founded in 1862 by Don Facundo Bacardí Massó in Cuba, the Bacardí company expanded into Puerto Rico in 1936 to increase sales in the United States. Since then, it has grown to be one of the biggest brands in the world.

The BACARDÍ Gran Reserva Diez is a blend of heavy rums (*aguardiente*) and light rum (*redistilado*) that has been barrel aged for 10 years. It gives rich oak, vanilla, caramel, and subtle notes of dried fruits, and is complex, smooth, and sophisticated.

DON Q GRAN RESERVA AÑEJO XO

40% ABV	MOLASSES	MODERN COLUMN STILL	DESTILERÍA SERRALLÉS

FLAVOUR

In 1865, the Serrallés family opened a rum-manufacturing plant at Hacienda Mercedita. In that same year, Juan Serrallés imported a still from France, which enabled him to produce his first casks of rum.

Don Q Gran Reserva XO is a blend of rums aged between nine and 12 years, and *solera* rums (see p87) matured up to 50 years. It has aromas of buttery oak, vanilla, and burnt caramel, with touches of leather, wood, and spicy coffee on the finish.

DOMINICAN REPUBLIC

Dominican rums are some of the most consumed in the Caribbean. Heavily influenced by the Cuban way of rum making, these light rums are popular worldwide.

WHAT MAKES DOMINICAN RUM UNIQUE?

The Dominican Republic has a protected designation of origin (PDO) for its rum. To qualify for the PDO "Ron Dominicano", producers must harvest their local sugarcane, and ferment, distil, and age the alcohol in oak barrels for a minimum of one year on the island.

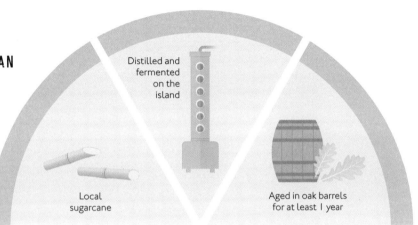

Local sugarcane

Distilled and fermented on the island

Aged in oak barrels for at least 1 year

TYPES OF DOMINICAN RUM

The Dominican Republic boasts a triumvirate of iconic rum brands, each representing the pinnacle of Dominican craftsmanship and tradition. Brugal stands as one of the oldest and most esteemed rum distilleries in the republic. Renowned for its distinctively woody, dry style, Brugal offers a range of expressions, from the youthful Brugal Añejo to the Brugal 1888, finished in sherry casks. Barceló has established itself as a symbol of Dominican elegance and sophistication. With a focus on making rums from cane juice, Barceló rums, such as Imperial and Imperial Premium Blend 30 Aniversario, showcase the country's sugarcane heritage and craftsmanship. Ron Bermúdez embodies the essence of the Dominican rum tradition. With a heritage spanning generations, Bermúdez rums are celebrated for their smoothness and complexity, exemplified by flagship rums like Bermúdez 1852 Aniversario.

MIXERS

FEVER-TREE Madagascan Cola
FRANKLIN & SONS Brewed Ginger Beer
LUSCOMBE Elderflower Bubbly

COCKTAILS

CUBA LIBRE see pp192–93
DAIQUIRI see pp194–95
PIÑA COLADA see pp210–11

OTHER RUMS TO TRY

RON BERMÚDEZ ANEJO SELECTO
RELICARIO RON DOMINICANO SUPREMO
RON MACORIX GRAN RESERVA

BARCELÓ IMPERIAL RUM

38% ABV	SUGARCANE JUICE	MODERN COLUMN STILL	RON BARCELÓ DISTILLERY

FLAVOUR

SWEET · SPICY · WOODY · HERBAL · RICH · FRUITY

A prize offering from Ron Barceló, this rum is distilled from local sugarcane juice and aged in American oak barrels. It delivers a rich and complex profile that reflects the four to 10 years of ageing in a tropical climate.

It exhibits a complex bouquet of caramel, vanilla, and tropical fruits. Its smooth, velvety palate unfolds with notes of chocolate, oak, and a hint of spice, culminating in a medium, satisfying finish.

BRUGAL 1888 DOBLEMENTE AÑEJADO

40% ABV	MOLASSES	MODERN COLUMN STILL	BRUGAL & CO.

FLAVOUR

SWEET · SPICY · WOODY · HERBAL · RICH · FRUITY

Launched in 2011 and paying homage to the year when Brugal began its journey, this rum melds together Brugal's rum-making heritage. It is crafted by the fifth generation of the Brugal family.

This blend of rums undergoes a double ageing process, first in American oak and then in sherry casks, a departure from traditional practices. It delivers a unique, dry profile, with notes of vanilla, red fruits, and toffee intertwined with cocoa and natural oak spice.

HAITI

Haiti is reputed to have dozens of micro-distilleries in the country making a sugarcane distillate called *clairin*. Like *rhum agricole*, it is also made from fresh cane juice. But is it *rhum*?

WHAT MAKES HAITIAN RUM UNIQUE?

Clairin is the spirit of Haiti and has been made the same way for hundreds of years, alongside traditional rum. Today, there are no guidelines for making Haitian rums, but they do adhere to the Caribbean Community (CARICOM) rum standard.

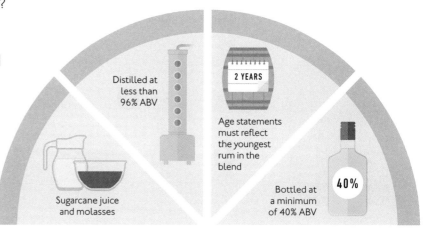

Distilled at less than 96% ABV

Sugarcane juice and molasses

2 YEARS

Age statements must reflect the youngest rum in the blend

Bottled at a minimum of 40% ABV

40%

TYPES OF HAITIAN RUM

The history of Haitian rum is a tale of resilience, innovation, and African heritage. It traces back to the island's colonial era, when sugarcane plantations flourished under French rule. As sugarcane became a vital commodity, rum production emerged as a significant industry in Haiti, creating wealth for many rum families. One of the most iconic names in Haitian rum history is Barbancourt. It came to symbolize the spirit of Haiti as rural *clairins* were rarely exported. Throughout the country's ups and downs, the Barbancourt rum brand has been a constant since 1862.

Rum remains an integral part of Haitian identity, culture, and economy. Today, Haiti's rum industry continues to evolve, with small-scale distilleries producing *clairin* and larger operations like Barbancourt exporting aged rums internationally, preserving the legacy of Haitian rum for generations to come.

MIXERS

FEVER-TREE Spiced Orange Ginger Ale

THREE CENTS Pink Grapefruit Soda

FRANKLIN & SONS Pineapple & Almond Soda

COCKTAILS

DAIQUIRI see pp194–95

EL PRESIDENTE

TI PUNCH (VIEUX) see p214

OTHER RUMS TO TRY

SAINT BENEVOLENCE RUM CLAIRIN

KLÉREN NASYONAL TRADITIONNEL 22

RHUM BARIK

RHUM BARBANCOURT RÉSERVE DU DOMAINE 15 YEARS

43% ABV	SUGARCANE JUICE	THREE-COLUMN CONTINUOUS STILL	SOCIÉTÉ DU RHUM BARBANCOURT

FLAVOUR

SWEET · SPICY · WOODY · HERBAL · RICH · FRUITY

Founded in 1862, Barbancourt is one of the oldest rum companies in the Caribbean. It makes this iconic rum from the juice of local, organic sugarcane called Madame Mevs.

Double distilled then aged in French oak casks, the "Cognac of Haiti" oozes flavours of raisins and apricots, hints of vanilla, oak, and touches of caramel, with a gentle sweetness. Layers on the palate include figs, prunes, toffee, a hint of spice, nuttiness, and citrus peel.

RHUM VIEUX LABBÉ 10 YEARS

43% ABV	SUGARCANE JUICE AND MOLASSES	TRADITIONAL COLUMN STILL	BERLING SA

FLAVOUR

SWEET · SPICY · WOODY · HERBAL · RICH · FRUITY

Rhum Vieux Labbé is exclusively produced in Haiti by members of the legendary Barbancourts, Haiti's most famous rum family.

Aged for a minimum of 10 years in French oak casks, this rum is made from both sugarcane juice and molasses, making it quite unique in the Caribbean. The resulting rum boasts flavours of floral notes, light orchard fruit, dark chocolate, oak, caramel, walnuts, honey, and vanilla, with a medium-dry finish.

GRENADA

Grenadian rums offer a unique blend of Caribbean flavours and know-how. From the fertile soil to traditional distillation, each sip embodies Grenada's essence.

WHAT MAKES GRENADIAN RUM UNIQUE?

The Spice Isle of the Caribbean is gaining recognition for its distinctive rums that encapsulate the island's lush *terroir* and rich cultural heritage. All rums are made in accordance to the Caribbean Community (CARICOM) rum standard.

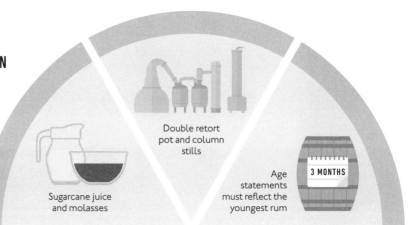

Sugarcane juice and molasses

Double retort pot and column stills

3 MONTHS

Age statements must reflect the youngest rum

TYPES OF GRENADIAN RUM

No strict rules govern what defines a Grenadian rum. Sugarcane juice and molasses are used in pot and column stills, and rum can be unaged or aged in wood.

Known for its fertile soil, Grenada produces sugarcane of exceptional quality. Brands like Renegade Rum are taking this a step further by making *terroir*-driven sugarcane juice rums, from various sugar estates on the island. Another prominent distillery is River Antoine Estate, renowned for its traditional, small-batch production methods. Its cane juice rums, distilled in antique pot stills fired by sugarcane husks, offer a glimpse into Grenada's rum-making past. Another notable producer is Clarke's Court, which has been distilling rum since 1937. Its No. 37 rum is perfect in a Mai Tai. But Grenada will always be known for its strong white rums at 69% ABV, like Westerhall's Jack Iron, Clarke's Court Pure White, and Rivers Royale export proof.

MIXERS

FEVER-TREE Mexican Lime Soda
THE LONDON ESSENCE Roasted Pineapple Crafted Soda
THREE CENTS Pink Grapefruit Soda

COCKTAILS

HURRICANE see pp198–99
RUM PUNCH see pp212–13
TI PUNCH see pp214–15

OTHER RUMS TO TRY

CLARKE'S COURT OLD GROG
WESTERHALL ESTATE 10XO
WESTERHALL ESTATE JACK IRON

RENEGADE DUNFERMLINE CANE RUM PRE-CASK POT STILL

50% ABV	SUGARCANE JUICE	DOUBLE RETORT POT STILL	RENEGADE RUM DISTILLERY

FLAVOUR

SWEET · SPICY · FRUITY · WOODY · RICH · HERBAL

The Renegade Rum Distillery was officially opened in 2022 to create *terroir*-driven rums from single sugarcane farms in Grenada.

The Dunfermline Pot Still is distilled from the juice of the Lacalome Red sugarcane, cultivated on a local farm. Unaged, this rum has aromas of green sugarcane, tropical fruit, and mint leaves, with flavours of butter, banana leaves, citrus oil, and sweet peppers.

RIVER ANTOINE ESTATE RIVERS ROYALE RUM

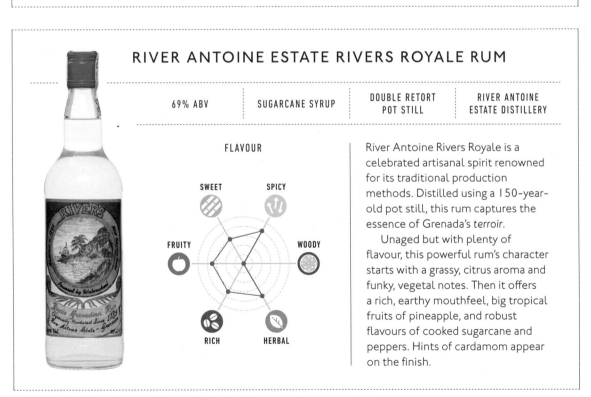

69% ABV	SUGARCANE SYRUP	DOUBLE RETORT POT STILL	RIVER ANTOINE ESTATE DISTILLERY

FLAVOUR

SWEET · SPICY · FRUITY · WOODY · RICH · HERBAL

River Antoine Rivers Royale is a celebrated artisanal spirit renowned for its traditional production methods. Distilled using a 150-year-old pot still, this rum captures the essence of Grenada's *terroir*.

Unaged but with plenty of flavour, this powerful rum's character starts with a grassy, citrus aroma and funky, vegetal notes. Then it offers a rich, earthy mouthfeel, big tropical fruits of pineapple, and robust flavours of cooked sugarcane and peppers. Hints of cardamom appear on the finish.

OTHER CARIBBEAN RUMS

The Caribbean is the epicentre of the rum world and the place where the spirit was born. A melting pot of styles, flavours, and *terroirs*, the region is a one-stop rum shop.

WHAT MAKES CARIBBEAN RUMS UNIQUE?

Distilleries across the Caribbean employ a variety of production methods, from double retort pot stills to multi-column stills, using cane juice or molasses and yielding rums with an array of flavours, from the bold and funky to the smooth and refined.

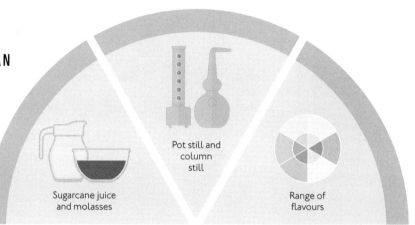

Sugarcane juice and molasses

Pot still and column still

Range of flavours

TYPES OF OTHER CARIBBEAN RUMS

Caribbean rum's uniqueness stems from its rich diversity of flavours, *terroirs*, and cultural influences. The rums offer a kaleidoscope of tastes deeply rooted in the islands' heritage and craftsmanship. Historical innovation has also influenced the various rum styles, including the use of multi-column stills (see p71) used to make rums like Angostura in Trinidad or Cruzan in the US Virgin Islands.

The use of local fresh sugarcane juice retains links to the natural environment, and this is portrayed in various rums from the French West Indies. Equally important is the use of regional molasses, which is imported from other parts of the Caribbean to islands where locally grown sugarcane is not enough to sustain a flourishing business, such as Antigua and St Lucia. Antigua's English Harbour and St Lucia's Chairman's Reserve rums, for example, are made from imported molasses.

MIXERS	COCKTAILS	OTHER RUMS TO TRY
TING Sparkling Grapefruit	**DAIQUIRI** see pp194–95	**BOUNTY PREMIUM GOLD** (St Lucia)
OLD JAMAICA Ginger Beer	**PIÑA COLADA** see pp210–11	**BRINLEY GOLD SHIPWRECK WHITE RUM** (St Kitts)
RUBICON Sparkling Lychee	**RUM PUNCH** see pp212–13	**CAVALIER ANTIGUA GOLD** (Antigua)

ANGOSTURA 1787

40% ABV	MOLASSES	MODERN COLUMN STILL	HOUSE OF ANGOSTURA

FLAVOUR

SWEET · SPICY · WOODY · HERBAL · RICH · FRUITY

To commemorate the building of the first sugar mill in Trinidad in 1787, this sweet-tasting rum is crafted by the renowned Angostura Distillery.

Aged for a minimum of 15 years in ex-bourbon barrels, this exceptional spirit delivers a rich and complex aroma profile of vanilla and ripe bananas, with a medium-bodied palate of hints of berries, prunes, and sweet oak notes. These flavours are intertwined with caramel and toffee nuances and a touch of leather.

CHAIRMAN'S RESERVE THE FORGOTTEN CASKS

40% ABV	MOLASSES	POT & TRADITIONAL COLUMN STILL	ST LUCIA DISTILLERS

FLAVOUR

SWEET · SPICY · WOODY · HERBAL · RICH · FRUITY

In 2007, a fire at the St Lucia Distillery nearly destroyed much of its warehouse. Fortunately, most of the casks were saved, but legend has it that a few casks were forgotten during the renovation of the new warehouse. Once found, the original liquid was blended and sold, so this new blend is a recreation of that smooth, old rum.

Rich, intense notes of raisins, honey, vanilla, and tobacco give way to a warm palate of cooked tropical fruit, walnuts, oak, and warm spices.

CRUZAN SINGLE BARREL

40% ABV	MOLASSES	MODERN MULTI-COLUMN STILL	CRUZAN RUM DISTILLERY

FLAVOUR

Part of the US Virgin Islands' local culture, this popular brand has a rich history dating back to 1760, and has been crafted by the Nelthropp family for eight generations.

The Cruzan Single Barrel is a unique blend of vintage rums aged between five and 12 years. The blended rums are matured in a single cask for a further year, creating a finished rum with notes of caramel, boiled sweets, citrus oils, toffee apple, and light oak.

ENGLISH HARBOUR RESERVE 10 YEARS

40% ABV	MOLASSES	TRADITIONAL THREE-COLUMN STILL	ANTIGUA DISTILLERY LTD

FLAVOUR

Formed in 1932, the Antigua Distillery Ltd has always made light- to medium-bodied rums in its column stills. Today, its blends are from a unique three-columned copper still, which continues the rum-making tradition.

This 10-year-old rum has essence of smoky oak with dried fruits, vanilla, citrus, and burnt sugar. The palate of coconut, cinnamon, and tropical florals is followed by a touch of mocha and baked apple.

SEVEN FATHOMS PREMIUM RUM

| 40% ABV | MOLASSES | HYBRID POT STILL | CAYMAN SPIRITS CO. DISTILLERY |

FLAVOUR

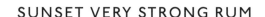

Crafted in batches in Grand Cayman, Seven Fathoms Premium Rum claims to be the only rum aged under the sea. In the past, when rums were transported by ship, some benefited from being accidentally aged. The ocean's movement helped force the rum into the pores of the wood, extracting woody flavours.

This hand-crafted rum is barrelled and anchored under water, where currents rock the liquid. This unique ageing process creates flavours of brown sugar, toffee, toasted almonds, and oak.

SUNSET VERY STRONG RUM

| 84.5% ABV | MOLASSES | MODERN TWIN-COLUMN STILL | ST VINCENT DISTILLERS LTD |

FLAVOUR

The most popular rum in St Vincent and one of the most potent rums by ABV on the market, Sunset Very Strong Rum is just that – strong. Bottled at a strength that would make most people sweat, this unaged white rum has much more going for it than just heat, lots of alcohol, and bragging rights.

Aromas of burnt sugar and almonds give way to scents of coconut shell. The palate is dry, then opens to raisins, desiccated coconut, and lime peel, finishing with ginger spice and white pepper.

MADEIRA

Madeira rum, also known as *"aguardente de cana"*, is a traditional spirit distilled from sugarcane juice on the Portuguese island of Madeira. It is officially permitted to use the term *"agrícola"* on the label.

WHAT MAKES MADEIRA RUM UNIQUE?

"Rum da Madeira" is a protected geographical indicator (GI). It is made through the fermentation and distillation of sugarcane juice from the island. It can be pot or column distilled, and ageing can only be carried out in oak casks for at least three years.

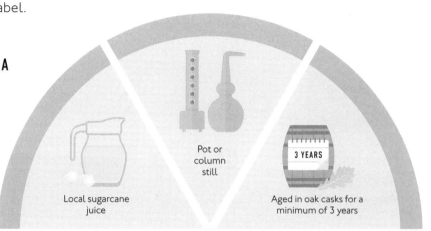

Local sugarcane juice

Pot or column still

3 YEARS

Aged in oak casks for a minimum of 3 years

TYPES OF MADEIRA RUM

Although the *rhum agricole* from Martinique, Guadeloupe, or even Réunion is better known, Madeira's *rum agrícola* has a small, but thriving market. There are six producers on the island, all making *agrícola* rums from local, freshly squeezed cane juice. The rums are aged predominantly in French oak, but various other wooden casks are now being used. Age statements are only in multiples of three years, so rum aged for four years must be labelled as 3 anos (3 years).

Madeira rum labelling:
- 6 anos or Reserva (Reserve)
- 12 anos or Reserva Antiga (Old Reserve)
- 15 anos or Reserva Especial (Special Reserve)
- 18 anos or Reserva Superior (Superior Reserve)
- 21 anos or Grande Reserva (Grand Reserve)
- 25 anos or Grande Reserva Premium (Grand Premium Reserve)

MIXERS

FEVER-TREE Mexican Lime Soda

THREE CENTS Pineapple Soda

FRANKLIN & SONS Brewed Ginger Beer

COCKTAILS

DAIQUIRI see pp194–95

HURRICANE see pp198–99

MAI TAI see pp202–03

OTHER RUMS TO TRY

970 RESERVA 6 ANOS

BALANCAL DOUBLE DISTILLED

CALHETA SELEÇÃO 1999

O REIZINHO 6 YEAR MADEIRA CASK

52.6% ABV	SUGARCANE JUICE	PORTUGUESE ALEMBIC (POT STILL)	O REIZINHO DISTILLERY

FLAVOUR

SWEET · SPICY · WOODY · HERBAL · RICH · FRUITY

Established in 1982, O Reizinho, which translates as "the little king", is a family-run distillery. All the rums produced at O Reizinho are distilled in a Portuguese alembic (pot still), then rested in stainless steel or aged in wooden casks.

This cask-strength six-year-old has been aged in Madeira casks, giving notes of wood, sugarcane, raisin, dark chocolate, and candied fruit. The palate offers flavours of sweet sugarcane, dry Madeira, dark fruit, and brown sugar.

WILLIAM HINTON 6 ANOS

40% ABV	SUGARCANE JUICE	TRADITIONAL COLUMN STILL	ENGENHO NOVO DA MADEIRA

FLAVOUR

SWEET · SPICY · WOODY · HERBAL · RICH · FRUITY

Made from freshly squeezed sugarcane juice, this Madeiran rum *agrícola* is distilled and aged for six years in French oak barrels. It is then decanted into five types of cask – bourbon, brandy, Madeira, port, and sherry – to be finished for an extra year.

The final product is a blend of these five cask finishes, creating a profile of fruit notes with toffee, hazelnuts, coffee, dry sherry, and spicy oak.

BRITAIN

In recent years, Scotland and England have witnessed a notable surge in the production of rums crafted from scratch, marking a significant shift in the spirits landscape.

WHAT MAKES BRITISH RUM UNIQUE?

There are no sugarcane fields in the British Isles, so molasses, sugarcane syrup, and even dehydrated sugarcane juice are imported to make rums from scratch. Various strains of yeast and local water are used in fermentation, as well as oak barrels for ageing.

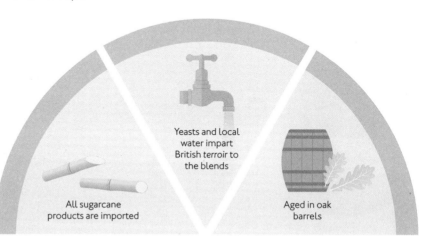

All sugarcane products are imported

Yeasts and local water impart British *terroir* to the blends

Aged in oak barrels

TYPES OF BRITISH RUMS

Traditionally renowned for their whisky and gin, British distilleries have embraced the challenge of rum production, capitalizing on their expertise in fermentation, distillation, and ageing.

In Scotland, distilleries such as Matugga and Ninefold have pioneered the creation of artisanal rums in a country that is world famous for its malts. These rums often showcase innovative approaches to fermentation and ageing, resulting in complex flavour profiles that rival some traditional Caribbean counterparts.

In England, a burgeoning craft rum scene has emerged, with brands like Scratch Rum, DropWorks, and Morvenna Rum leading the charge. Two Drifters rums are made with a carbon negative footprint to increase sustainability. These producers prioritize quality ingredients and small-batch production methods, infusing their rums with regional influences and a sense of British *terroir*.

MIXERS

LUSCOMBE Passionate Ginger Beer

CHEGWORTH VALLEY Cloudy Apple Juice

FEVER-TREE Spiced Orange Ginger Ale

COCKTAILS

DARK 'N' STORMY see pp196–97

MOJITO see pp206–07

TREACLE

OTHER RUMS TO TRY

MORVENNA CORNISH WHITE RUM

ROSEMULLION GOLD RUM

HURRICANE OVERPROOF

MANX RUM

DROPWORKS FUNK DROP RUM

63% ABV	SUGARCANE HONEY	DOUBLE RETORT POT STILL	DROPWORKS DISTILLERY, ENGLAND

FLAVOUR

SWEET · SPICY · FRUITY · WOODY · RICH · HERBAL

As one of Britain's newest rum makers, this Nottinghamshire distillery imports sugarcane honey and ferments using three strains of yeast to make this funky, overproof rum.

It is triple distilled using techniques associated with high-ester Jamaican rums, creating an explosion of tropical flavours such as cooked pineapple, guava jelly, coconut, herbs, and a touch of nail polish remover. On the palate, there is a hot blend of sweetness quickly fading into a touch of earthiness, with more fruit and white pepper on the finish.

MATUGGA MAVUNO RUM 2022 RELEASE #2

48% ABV	MOLASSES	HYBRID POT STILL	MATUGGA DISTILLERY, SCOTLAND

FLAVOUR

SWEET · SPICY · FRUITY · WOODY · RICH · HERBAL

Mavuno, meaning "harvest" in Swahili, is made from imported Ugandan molasses and crafted in Scotland. This 100 per cent pot-stilled rum is the second single-cask release from the Matugga Distillery, founded in 2018.

The rum has been aged for three years in American oak that has previously aged bourbon and subsequently Cognac. A floral, fruity aroma accompanies a palate of orchard fruit like green apples and pear drops, plus butterscotch and dried fruit, with a finish of smoke, spicy wood, and sweet peppers.

NINEFOLD CASK AGED PURE SINGLE RUM

45% ABV	MOLASSES	HYBRID POT STILL	NINEFOLD DISTILLERY, SCOTLAND

FLAVOUR

The southwest of Scotland is not known for its rum making, but the Ninefold Distillery is quickly changing that. Rum production started in 2019 with its first batches made from imported molasses.

The rum is matured for at least 18 months in ex-bourbon barrels to give aromas of orchard fruit, allspice, and cedarwood. The palate brings warm flavours of sweet caramel, butterscotch, toffee, dark chocolate, vanilla, and oak, with a finish that is mellow and rounded.

1812 3 YEAR OLD AGED RUM

43% ABV	DEHYDRATED SUGARCANE JUICE	SINGLE POT STILL	PORTSMOUTH DISTILLERY, ENGLAND

FLAVOUR

Matured at the historical Fort Cumberland, in the naval city of Portsmouth, this rum has been aged in ex-bourbon barrels for three years. The distillery is only 100 metres (110 yards) from the sea, so the local salty marine environment is thought to aid in flavour development of this lightly aged rum.

On the nose, there is a subtle grassiness, with hints of mixed herbs and citrus. The palate has light flavours of burnt caramel, toffee, vanilla ice cream, and oak.

SCRATCH RUM SINGLE CASK RELEASE WINTER 2023

| 47.2% ABV | MOLASSES | COPPER POT STILL | SCRATCH DISTILLERY, ENGLAND |

FLAVOUR

SWEET · SPICY · FRUITY · WOODY · RICH · HERBAL

Scratch Distillery opened its doors to the world in 2016. This special 2023 release is the first in a series of rums drawn from a single barrel that was matured in the distillery's Hertfordshire warehouse.

This double distilled rum has been aged for three years in an ex-muscat cask, made from French oak. It has warm aromas of Christmas cake, orange peel, and vanilla, with a medium-long palate of toffee, butterscotch, treacle, nutmeg, cloves, oak, and a touch of liquorice.

TWO DRIFTERS SIGNATURE RUM

| 40% ABV | MOLASSES | SINGLE POT STILL | TWO DRIFTERS DISTILLERY, ENGLAND |

FLAVOUR

SWEET · SPICY · FRUITY · WOODY · RICH · HERBAL

This light, dry rum is made in the UK's first rum distillery to have a carbon negative footprint. In the journey from sugarcane grass to the customer's glass, the distillery removes more carbon dioxide than it creates.

Distilled in an electrically powered pot still, the rum benefits from being lightly aged in ex-Madeira casks, which add a touch of colour, aroma, and texture to the mouth. Touches of orange, honey, and ripe bananas linger on the tongue, with a medium finish of liquorice and spice.

GUYANA

Although the Diamond Distillery is the only distillery left in Guyana, this living rum museum has the production power to craft many styles of long-forgotten rum.

WHAT MAKES GUYANESE RUM UNIQUE?

The Demerara region, where the Diamond Distillery is located, has geographical indication (GI) protection, so Demerara rum must be fermented, distilled, and aged in Demerara. Pot and column stills can both be used, and any age claim must designate the youngest rum.

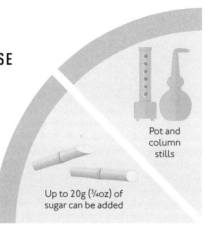

Pot and column stills

Up to 20g (¾oz) of sugar can be added

Fermented, distilled, and aged in Demerara

An age claim must refer to the youngest rum

3 YEARS

TYPES OF GUYANESE RUM

Guyanese rums have been celebrated for over 300 years for their artisanal approach and quality. These rums have also been the backbone for navy rum blends over the years. However, El Dorado rums are the most famous to carry the Demerara name.

Demerara rum types are as follows:
- **Demerara rum** Unblended or blended, but not blended with alcohol produced outside the geographical area.
- **Old Demerara rum** Unblended or blended, aged for a minimum of two years, and not blended with alcohol produced outside the geographical area.

- **Cask aged Demerara rum** Unblended or blended rum aged for a minimum of three years.
- **Special reserve Demerara rum** Unblended or blended rum aged for a minimum of 12 years.
- **Grand special reserve Demerara rum** Unblended or blended rum aged for a minimum of 25 years.

MIXERS	COCKTAILS	OTHER RUMS TO TRY
GUNNER SAINT Ginger Beer	**DARK 'N' STORMY** see pp196–97	**XM ROYAL 10 YEARS**
FENTIMANS Ginger Ale	**MAI TAI** see pp202–03	**DEMERARA SUPERIOR HIGH WINE**
THE LONDON ESSENCE Roasted Crafted Pineapple Soda	**RUM MANHATTAN**	**DEMERARA DIAMOND RESERVE GOLD**

EL DORADO SPECIAL RESERVE 15 YEAR OLD

43% ABV	MOLASSES	POT & COLUMN STILLS	DIAMOND DISTILLERY

FLAVOUR

The Diamond Distillery, owned by Demerara Distillers Ltd, is home to some of the world's oldest and unique rum stills. In fact, it has two pot stills and a column still made partly from wood.

These historic pieces of equipment are used to help craft this iconic 15-year-old rum. It boasts flavours of chocolate, candied orange, almonds, pineapple, rich coffee, vanilla, sweet peppers, and smoky oak.

SKIPPER RUM

40% ABV	MOLASSES	POT & COLUMN STILLS	DIAMOND DISTILLERY

FLAVOUR

When rum drinkers think of dark, navy-styled rums, they think of the ocean, the Royal Navy, and the rum ration, and Skipper Rum is one of the brands that always comes to mind.

A classic dark rum in appearance, this product of Guyana gets its colour from the addition of caramel. On the nose, there are hints of espresso bean, raisins, cacao, and toasted oak. The palate has flavours of treacle, toffee, and butterscotch.

VENEZUELA

Made in South America, but with an essence of the Caribbean, Venezuelan rums are truly one of the most versatile categories of rums that will ever grace your glass.

WHAT MAKES VENEZUELAN RUM UNIQUE?

Rum from Venezuela must be made from Venezuelan sugarcane juice, syrup, or molasses, distilled in either pot or column stills, aged for a minimum of two years in oak, and bottled between 40% and 50% ABV. Sweetening is permitted.

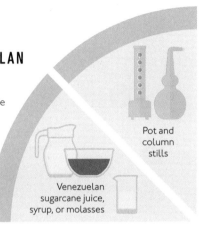

Venezuelan sugarcane juice, syrup, or molasses

Pot and column stills

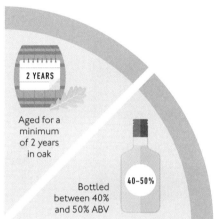

2 YEARS

Aged for a minimum of 2 years in oak

40–50%

Bottled between 40% and 50% ABV

TYPES OF VENEZUELAN RUM

Venezuelan rum encompasses a spectrum of styles, from light and fruity to rich, sweet, and complex. Brands like Diplomático offer a full range of expressions, including the unique Planas, which is a white rum aged from two to six years and filtered through carbon.

Premium Venezuelan rums are often enjoyed neat or on the rocks to fully savour their nuanced flavours. A twist of orange peel added to a Ron Carúpano 12 Year Old or Pampero Aniversario, for example, adds an extra dimension to the drink. Venezuelan rums also shine in more elaborate concoctions, adding layers of

complexity to drinks like an Old Fashioned or Rum Manhattan. Santa Teresa 1796 is perfect for cocktails such as these, as the medium-bodied rum pairs well with sweet and spicy flavours.

With their versatility and quality, Venezuelan rums appeal to casual drinkers and seasoned aficionados alike.

MIXERS

LUSCOMBE Passionate Ginger Beer
SEKFORDE Lime, Mint, & Cacao Soda
FEVER-TREE White Grape & Apricot Soda

COCKTAILS

DAIQUIRI see pp194–95
MAI TAI see pp202–03
MARY PICKFORD see pp204–05

OTHER RUMS TO TRY

PAMPERO ANIVERSARIO
RON CARÚPANO 12 YEAR OLD
CACIQUE 500 RON EXTRA AÑEJO

DIPLOMÁTICO RESERVA EXCLUSIVA

40% ABV	MOLASSES	DOUBLE RETORT POT & COLUMN STILL	DESTILERÍAS UNIDAS SA (DUSA)

FLAVOUR

The DUSA distillery is renowned for making many rum brands, and the Diplomático Reserva Exclusiva is one of the most popular. A blend of rums made from molasses, it is a marriage of both pot and column still distillates.

After ageing these rums from two to 12 years in American oak barrels, the rum is then doused with a little rum syrup to round off the flavour. Expect a profile of banoffee pie, caramel, cocoa, demerara sugar, coffee, and light oak.

SANTA TERESA 1796

40% ABV	MOLASSES & SUGARCANE HONEY	MULTI-COLUMN & POT STILL	HACIENDA SANTA TERESA

FLAVOUR

This single-estate rum is Venezuela's oldest rum brand, dating back to 1796. It is a blend of column and pot still rums aged between four and 35 years.

The rums are then re-aged by the *solera* method (see p87), which slowly marries some of the oldest rums at the distillery with new blends, transforming them into a single rum. This method ensures consistency and balance, and the rum oozes a flavour profile of cooked bananas, pecan pie, walnuts, oak, and caramel.

WIDER SOUTH AMERICA

If *cachaça* is the biggest spirit in South America, then rum is a close second. From Venezuela to Argentina, and from Peru to Colombia, this sugarcane distillate stays true to its cultural roots.

WHAT MAKES SOUTH AMERICAN RUM UNIQUE?

Although each country in South America has its own legal definition of what rum is, they all agree that it must be distilled in pot or column stills and made from a byproduct of sugarcane (usually molasses).

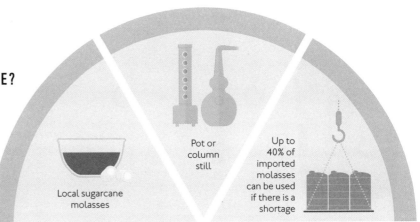

Local sugarcane molasses

Pot or column still

Up to 40% of imported molasses can be used if there is a shortage

TYPES OF SOUTH AMERICAN RUM

In South America, the common spirit is *aguardiente de caña* (cane liquor) or sugarcane brandy. Most people will also call this rum. But throughout South America, *aguardiente* and rum sit side by side on shelves, with the former unaged and raw, and the latter usually made from molasses and aged in oak.

Venezuela (see pp162–63) has a booming rum industry, with a registered geographical indication (GI) to protect its rums. Some countries have a history of making and drinking cultural and ancestral heritage cane spirits, such as *cañazo* (Peru) and *viche* (Colombia). Both have undoubtedly influenced rum brands such as Ron Millonario (Peru) and La Hechicera (Colombia) in local markets. If you want to explore South America through your palate, try brands such as Espinillar Gran Reserva 20 Years (Uruguay), Isla Ñ (Argentina), and Ron Viejo de Caldas (Colombia).

MIXERS

LUSCOMBE Passionate Ginger Beer
HARTRIDGES Cloudy Apple Juice
FEVER-TREE Spiced Orange Ginger Ale

COCKTAILS

DAIQUIRI see pp194–95
MOJITO see pp206–07
RUM MANHATTAN

OTHER RUMS TO TRY

ISLA Ñ RESERVE GOLD (Argentina)
RHUM TOUCAN BOCO (French Guiana)
RON CARTAVIO XO (Peru)

BORGOE 8 YEAR OLD

40% ABV	MOLASSES	THREE-COLUMN STILL	SURINAME ALCOHOLIC BEVERAGES NV

FLAVOUR

Suriname, a burgeoning rum-producing nation, has slowly gained recognition for its distinctive spirits, especially in European countries like the Netherlands. As a relatively young player in the industry, Suriname's tropical climate helps its rums to mature quickly, resulting in full-flavoured examples.

Among these is the Borgoe 8 Year Old. Its smooth blend boasts rich notes of burnt caramel, candied orange, molasses, vanilla, and spices, which showcase the country's unique *terroir*.

LA HECHICERA RESERVA FAMILIAR

40% ABV	MOLASSES	MULTI-COLUMN STILL	CASA SANTANA RON Y LICORES SAS

FLAVOUR

Although this rum is a blend of distillates predominantly from the Caribbean and Central America, it is blended and aged entirely in Barranquilla, Colombia.

This medium-bodied rum is matured between 12 and 21 years in a *solera*-style system (see p87), and the movement of liquid from one layer to another helps to create a harmonious consistency in flavour. It has aromas of leather, vanilla, and light wood, with a complex palate of creamy wood, butterscotch, and oak, and a touch of bitterness on the finish.

UNITED STATES

The United States is considered to be one of the world's biggest consumers of rum. Although 70 per cent of rum drunk is from US territories like Puerto Rico, mainland rums are becoming popular again.

WHAT MAKES AMERICAN RUM UNIQUE?

In the US, rum is defined as a spirit distilled from the fermented juice of sugarcane, sugarcane syrup, sugarcane molasses, or other sugarcane byproducts. It must be bottled at a minimum of 40% ABV and have the taste, aroma, and characteristics generally attributed to rum.

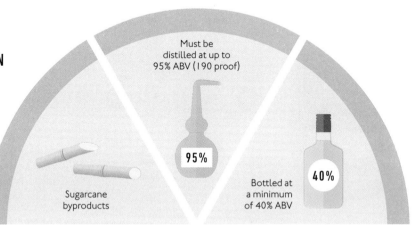

Sugarcane byproducts

Must be distilled at up to 95% ABV (190 proof)

95%

Bottled at a minimum of 40% ABV

40%

TYPES OF AMERICAN RUM

Although it is one of the biggest consumers of rum, the United States doesn't recognize any of the geographical indicators (GIs) that have been created worldwide to protect various rum trademarks from being exploited. This means terms like "agricole" can be labelled on a rum from Hawaii made from fresh sugarcane juice, or a rum from the Carolinas can be called "Jamerican Rum" to imitate a true Jamaican rum.

A new wave of US craft distillers is seeking to make rums that can sit side by side with their Caribbean counterparts on the world stage. In New York City, you'll find Owney's Original New York City Rum. Hand crafted from US molasses, it is bold and complex and works well in a Daiquiri or light Rum Punch. From Ipswich, Massachusetts, the Privateer Distillery is making New England rums from a bygone era, which are rich, flavoursome, and perfect neat or in a Mai Tai.

MIXERS

THREE CENTS Pink Grapefruit Soda
FRANKLIN & SONS Pineapple & Almond Soda
DOUBLE DUTCH Ginger Ale

COCKTAILS

DAIQUIRI see pp194–95
MOJITO see pp206–07
RUM MANHATTAN

OTHER RUMS TO TRY

PRIVATEER NAVY YARD
RICHLAND CLASSIC RESERVE
OWNEY'S ORIGINAL NEW YORK CITY RUM

BAYOU MARDI GRAS XO

40% ABV	MOLASSES	COPPER POT STILL	BAYOU RUM DISTILLERY

FLAVOUR

The Bayou Rum Distillery, in Louisiana, opened its doors in 2013 with the premise to remind Americans that, historically, they enjoyed rum before they enjoyed whiskey. Its rums are hand crafted in pot stills and aged in predominantly ex-bourbon casks.

The Mardi Gras XO is slightly different in that it is aged for up to six years in a *solera* system (see p87) and then finished for an extra year in Pedro Ximenez sherry casks. The rum gives floral notes of stone fruits, honey, sherry, peppers, and spicy oak.

MONTANYA VALENTIA

40% ABV	MOLASSES	CUSTOM POT STILL	MONTANYA DISTILLERS

FLAVOUR

Montanya Distillers, in Colorado, make rum in the Rocky Mountains at nearly 2,700 metres (9,000 feet) above sea level. They distil a fermented wash made from molasses imported from Louisiana. The ageing of all their rums takes place in local Colorado ex-whiskey barrels.

The Valentia spends four years in these barrels before being finished in rye whiskey casks for six to 12 weeks. It has flavours of vanilla, cinnamon, nutmeg, ginger, and cardamom, with a honeyed floral, black pepper, and spiced oak finish.

MEXICO

In recent years, there has been a growing interest in Mexican rum, with some distilleries focusing on crafting high-quality expressions that showcase the country's unique *terroir* and flavours.

WHAT MAKES MEXICAN RUM UNIQUE?

Mexican rum must be made from locally grown sugarcane, the distillate must be aged for six months to be called rum, and for one year to be called aged rum. Flavourings and sweetening are permitted. Rum must be bottled between 35% and 55% ABV.

Aged for at least 6 months, and 1 year for aged rum

Locally grown sugarcane

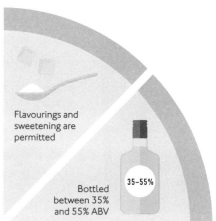

Flavourings and sweetening are permitted

35–55%

Bottled between 35% and 55% ABV

TYPES OF MEXICAN RUM

The words "Mexico" and "alcohol" may make you think of tequila and mezcal, but rum and sugarcane spirits have been made in the country for centuries. Up until the late 18th century, the production of rum and other local spirits was banned by the Spanish government, which wanted to protect the sales of imported Spanish brandy. The locals didn't pay much heed and still made *aguardiente de caña*, or *ron chinguirito*, in the remote hills as a mark of defiance.

While Mexican rum may not yet have the same recognition and reputation as rums from other countries, its producers are working to elevate its status and carve out a niche in the competitive world of rum production. As a footnote, Mexico does have a geographical indication (GI) for a sugarcane distillate called *charanda*. It is made exclusively in Michoacan and was granted a protected designation of origin (PDO) in 2003.

MIXERS	COCKTAILS	OTHER RUMS TO TRY
FEVER-TREE Mexican Lime Soda	**DAIQUIRI** see pp194–95	**CAMAZOTZ OAXACAN RUM**
THE LONDON ESSENCE Roasted Pineapple Crafted Soda	**HURRICANE** see pp198–99	**GUSTOSO ARTISANAL MEXICAN RUM**
TING Grapefruit Soda	**MOJITO** see pp206–07	**TSO'OK RUM REPOSADO**

DAKABEND

| 49% ABV | SUGARCANE JUICE | POT STILL | TOSBA DISTILLERY |

FLAVOUR

SWEET · SPICY · WOODY · HERBAL · RICH · FRUITY

"Dakabend" loosely means "the disobedient one" in homage to the rum maker's family journey in the spirits industry. Made in San Cristóbal Lachirioag in Oaxaca, the local sugarcane is freshly pressed then wild fermented in wooden vats within hours of harvest.

The long fermentation, which can last one to two weeks, creates funky esters that are concentrated in a wood-fired mezcal pot still. It has flavours of fresh sugarcane, green banana, dried herbs, and green olives, with a long, sweet, and savoury finish.

PARANUBES

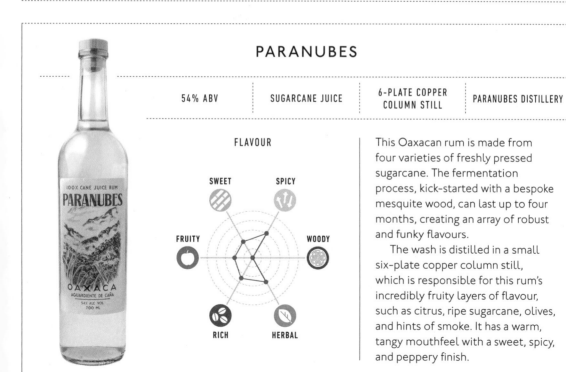

| 54% ABV | SUGARCANE JUICE | 6-PLATE COPPER COLUMN STILL | PARANUBES DISTILLERY |

FLAVOUR

SWEET · SPICY · WOODY · HERBAL · RICH · FRUITY

This Oaxacan rum is made from four varieties of freshly pressed sugarcane. The fermentation process, kick-started with a bespoke mesquite wood, can last up to four months, creating an array of robust and funky flavours.

The wash is distilled in a small six-plate copper column still, which is responsible for this rum's incredibly fruity layers of flavour, such as citrus, ripe sugarcane, olives, and hints of smoke. It has a warm, tangy mouthfeel with a sweet, spicy, and peppery finish.

CENTRAL AMERICA

Although Central America (except Belize) shares a common language, Spanish, the rums from the region are varied and distinct, each one capturing the heart and soul of its history, culture, and spirit of the local people.

WHAT MAKES CENTRAL AMERICAN RUM UNIQUE?

These rums tend to be light bodied and made in column stills. They must be made from local molasses, cane juice, or sugarcane syrup and distilled to less than 96% ABV. *Aguardiente* must be aged in wood for at least two years to be classified as rum.

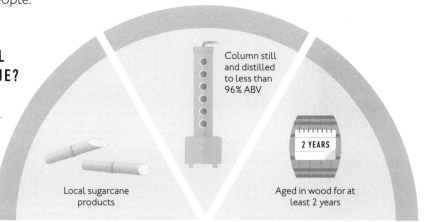

Local sugarcane products

Column still and distilled to less than 96% ABV

2 YEARS

Aged in wood for at least 2 years

TYPES OF CENTRAL AMERICAN RUM

The rums from the seven countries in Central America are a medley of taste, flavour, and style. They boast a rich history that is tangled with the region's colonial past. It dates back to the Spanish conquest, when sugarcane cultivation flourished and provided the foundation for rum production that continues to thrive today.

In Guatemala, Botran rums are aged high in the mountains and are renowned for their complexity. Nicaragua's Flor de Caña embodies the country's volcanic *terroir* and meticulous ageing process. Panama rums, like Abuelo, are medium bodied, fruity, and perfect for cocktails like El Presidente.

Central American rums, with their diverse expressions, offer a captivating journey through the region's cultural heritage and natural abundance. Whether enjoyed neat or in cocktails, they embody the spirit of the tropics and the artistry of centuries-old traditions.

MIXERS	COCKTAILS	OTHER RUMS TO TRY
COCA-COLA Vanilla **DOUBLE DUTCH** Cranberry & Ginger Tonic **FEVER-TREE** Spiced Orange Ginger Ale	**DAIQUIRI** see pp194–95 **MOJITO** see pp206–07 **RUM MANHATTAN**	**COPALLI BARREL RESTED RUM** (Belize) **RON CORTEZ 3 YEAR OLD** (Panama) **RON ZACAPA AMBAR 12** (Guatemala)

BOTRAN 18 SOLERA 1893

40% ABV	SUGARCANE SYRUP	MULTI-COLUMN STILL	INDUSTRIAS LICORERAS DE GUATEMALA

FLAVOUR

SWEET · SPICY · WOODY · HERBAL · RICH · FRUITY

Ron Botran 18 is a premium Guatemalan rum that has been a flagship for the brand for a number of years. Made from locally sourced sugarcane syrup, the rums in this blend are between five and 18 years old, and are dynamically aged in an adapted *solera* system (see p87) that includes ex-bourbon barrels, sherry casks, and port barrels.

This complex rum boasts a flavour profile of warm vanilla, caramel, dark chocolate, sherry, dark berries, and oak.

CIHUATÁN INDIGO AGED 8 YEARS

40% ABV	MOLASSES	MULTI-COLUMN STILL	LICORERA CIHUATÁN

FLAVOUR

SWEET · SPICY · WOODY · HERBAL · RICH · FRUITY

Founded in 2004, Ron Cihuatán is the first rum brand to be exported internationally from El Salvador. Inspired by Mayan folklore and the colour blue, Indigo is a blend of light and heavy rums from column stills, which are aged for a minimum of eight years in American white oak barrels that were previously used to age bourbon.

It boasts notes of vanilla-flavoured cappuccino, with a creamy, nutty texture, and hints of hazelnuts, almond, spices like lemongrass, and sweet peppers, with a medium finish.

DON OMARIO'S VINTAGE RUM AGED 10 YEARS

40% ABV	MOLASSES	TRIPLE COLUMN STILL	TRAVELLERS LIQUORS LTD

FLAVOUR

Produced at the Travellers Distillery in Belmopan, Belize, this double-distilled 10-year-old rum was launched to honour the legacy of Don Omario Perdomo, founder of the rum distillery in 1953.

The rum is aged predominantly in ex-bourbon barrels at the warehouses in the subtropical climate of Belize City. Ageing helps this rum to acquire flavours of butterscotch, chocolate, coffee, soft fruits like prunes, dried apricots, and dates. The finish brings oak and dried vanilla pods, with hints of sweet peppers and allspice.

FLOR DE CAÑA 12

40% ABV	MOLASSES	MULTI-COLUMN STILL	COMPAÑÍA LICORERA DE NICARAGUA

FLAVOUR

Flor de Caña, meaning "cane flower", is made at one of the only rum distilleries in the world that is certified carbon neutral and fair trade. It uses 100 per cent renewable energy to make its rums.

This Nicaraguan light rum is continuously distilled and aged in ex-bourbon barrels for a minimum of 12 years. The rum is dry with subtle aromas of toffee, cinnamon, dusty cocoa, and apples, with a finish of oak and pepper.

RON ABUELO AÑEJO 12 AÑOS

40% ABV	MOLASSES & SUGARCANE JUICE	COLUMN STILL	VARELA HERMANOS SA

FLAVOUR

Varela Hermanos is one of the few rum distilleries still to use molasses produced locally from estate-grown cane. First produced in 1960, Abuelo, which means "grandfather" in Spanish, is a light- to medium-bodied Panamanian rum that typifies the regional style of light to medium rums loved by locals.

Aged for a minimum of 12 years, it boasts flavours of caramel, dates, brown sugar, candied orange, allspice, nutmeg, and cocoa, with a light, sweet, oaky finish.

RON CENTENARIO 20 ANIVERSARIO FUNDACIÓN

40% ABV	MOLASSES	MULTI COLUMN STILL	CENTENARIO INTERNACIONAL SA

FLAVOUR

The Centenario Internacional Distillery in Costa Rica originally bottled whisky from Scotland, so it started to age its rums in ex-Scotch whisky barrels. It also employs a *solera* ageing method (see p87) for its older rums, which tend to be on the sweeter side.

The Centenario 20 Aniversario Fundación, one of the first rums to be exported from Costa Rica, has sweet aromas of vanilla, maraschino cherry, and ripened pineapple. The palate is creamy with more fruit, wood, sticky toffee, butterscotch, and spice.

AUSTRALIA

Rum has a long history in Australia. In recent times, the country has welcomed a range of craft distilleries producing high-quality boutique rums, which draw inspiration from local ingredients and techniques to create unique expressions that reflect Australia's rich rum heritage.

WHAT MAKES AUSTRALIAN RUM UNIQUE?

All Australian rums must be made from a byproduct of sugarcane, and possess the taste, aroma, and other characteristics generally attributed to rum. The distillate must be aged in wood for a minimum of two years and can be bottled at a strength no lower than 37% ABV.

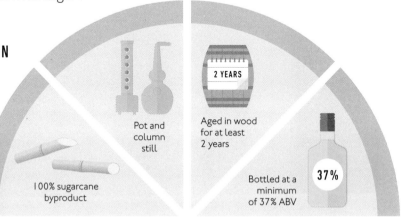

100% sugarcane byproduct

Pot and column still

2 YEARS

Aged in wood for at least 2 years

Bottled at a minimum of 37% ABV

37%

TYPES OF AUSTRALIAN RUM

In Australia, 95 per cent of all sugarcane is grown in Queensland (the other 5 per cent is grown in New South Wales). Even so, Australian rums encompass a diverse array of styles. Most rums are made from molasses and aged in various types of barrels, casks, and vats. The biggest of these brands is the iconic Bundaberg, which offers a range of expressions from its classic dark rum to limited-edition releases. Beenleigh Rum presents a line-up of handcrafted rums that celebrate traditional techniques and local ingredients.

Although rum in Australia has to be stored in wood for a minimum of two years to be legally sold as rum, the Husk rum brand has now trademarked the term "Australian cultivated rum" (ACR). ACR rums must be made from 100 per cent fresh cane juice of known cane varieties that grow in a recognized region between Grafton, New South Wales, and Mossman, Queensland.

MIXERS	COCKTAILS	OTHER RUMS TO TRY
BUNDABERG Ginger Beer	**DAIQUIRI** see pp194–95	**PREMIUM ORD RIVER**
SEKFORDE Lime, Mint, & Cacao Soda	**DARK 'N' STORMY** see pp196–97	**INNER CIRCLE NAVY STRENGTH**
TING Grapefruit Soda	**MOJITO** see pp206–07	**ARCHIE ROSE TRIPLE MOLASSES**

BEENLEIGH ARTISAN DISTILLERS DOUBLE CASK

40% ABV	MOLASSES	POT & COLUMN STILL	BEENLEIGH DISTILLERY

FLAVOUR

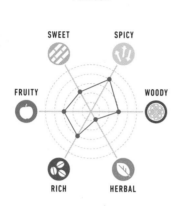

Beenleigh Distillery is one of Australia's oldest rum distilleries, producing premium rum using traditional methods and locally sourced ingredients.

Its Double Cask Rum is distilled in both column and pot stills, and takes advantage of resting for five years in historic kauri pine vats, Australian brandy vats, and ex-bourbon barrels. The result is a complex rum with aromas and flavours of fruit and berry notes, sweet allspice, and a long palate of molasses, vanilla bean, oak, and more spice.

HUSK SIGNATURE ACR

41.8% ABV	SUGARCANE JUICE	SINGLE POT STILL	HUSK FARM DISTILLERY

FLAVOUR

This Signature Rum is the first official Australian cultivated rum (ACR) by the Husk Distillery. A "farm to bottle" rum, it's made from 100 per cent single-estate cane juice, with no added flavours, colours, or sweeteners and is non-chill filtered.

The warm, subtropical climate where this rum is aged helps it to mature quickly in American oak barrels. It oozes flavours of light, spicy oak with hints of dried and tropical fruits like pineapple. These lead to a herbal, grassy, earthy finish with a touch of tobacco leaf.

ASIA

Some the world's biggest rum brands are made
and consumed in the Asian region. That makes
perfect sense as sugarcane and the beverages
connected to it have been consumed
in Asia for thousands of years.

WHAT MAKES ASIAN RUM UNIQUE?

Asian rum brands are rarely seen
outside their local markets and
they have a loyal domestic
following. The popular brands
are industrially produced in
multi-column stills and made
from molasses, with caramel
and sugar added to satisfy
the local palate.

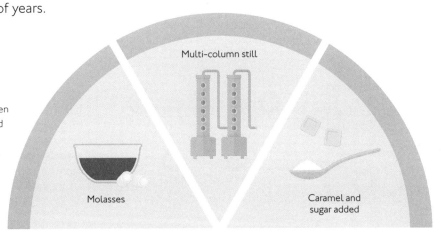

Multi-column still

Molasses

Caramel and
sugar added

TYPES OF ASIAN RUM

As you explore the world of
Asian rums, you'll encounter a
fascinating array of flavours and
traditions, each bottle telling a
story of heritage and innovation.
From the vibrant streets of
Bangkok to the tranquil shores of
Bali, Asian rums invite you on a
journey of sensory delight and
cultural discovery. The Philippines
boasts the world's biggest selling
rum, Tanduay, celebrated locally
for its bold and robust character.
In Phuket, Thailand, you'll discover
the exquisite flavours of Chalong
Bay, inspired by French Armagnac,
in which fresh sugarcane juice wine
is distilled like a sugarcane brandy,
offering aromatic tastes and
flavours. In Japan, Ryoma Rum
captivates with its delicate balance
of sweetness and complexity,
reflecting the country's dedication
to precision and refinement. India's
Old Monk Rum stands as a beloved
icon, with its rich history and
distinctive vanilla undertones
captivating enthusiasts worldwide.

MIXERS

LUSCOMBE Ginger Beer
THE LONDON ESSENCE Roasted
Pineapple Crafted Soda
FEVER-TREE Madagascan Cola

COCKTAILS

DARK 'N' STORMY see pp196–97
MOJITO see pp206–07
RUM PUNCH see pp212–13

OTHER RUMS TO TRY

CAMIKARA 12YO (India)
ROCKLAND WHITE RUM
(Sri Lanka)
SANGSOM (Thailand)

CHALONG BAY DOUBLE BARREL

47% ABV	SUGARCANE JUICE	COPPER ARMAGNAC COLUMN STILL	CHALONG BAY DISTILLERY

FLAVOUR

SWEET · SPICY · WOODY · HERBAL · RICH · FRUITY

Made from 100 per cent local Thai sugarcane juice, this sweet-tasting rum captures the local *terroir* in abundance. After being distilled in a small French Armagnac still, it is rested in stainless steel for six months. Then some of the rum is put into French oak barrels, while the rest goes into ex-Armagnac casks. After 18 months, the two rums are blended.

The marriage of the two barrels boasts flavours of freshly cut sugarcane, light, oaky vanilla, and clove, with tropical fruits, apricots, cinnamon, and spice.

CORONATION KHUKRI RUM

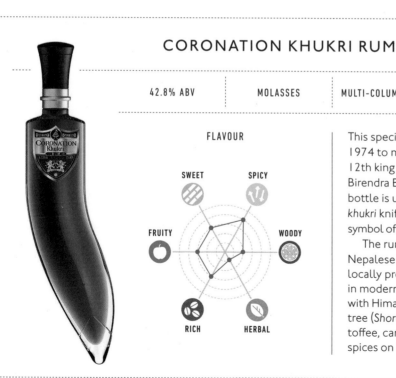

42.8% ABV	MOLASSES	MULTI-COLUMN STILL	THE NEPAL DISTILLERIES PRIVATE LIMITED

FLAVOUR

SWEET · SPICY · WOODY · HERBAL · RICH · FRUITY

This special rum was launched in 1974 to mark the coronation of the 12th king of Nepal, the late King Birendra Bir Bikram Shah Dev. The bottle is uniquely shaped like a *khukri* knife, which is a national symbol of pride, bravery, and elegance.

The rum is a celebration of Nepalese heritage. It is made from locally produced molasses, distilled in modern column stills, blended with Himalayan water, and aged in sal tree (*Shorea robusta*) barrels. Expect toffee, caramel, treacle, and sweet spices on the palate.

KIYOMI JAPANESE RUM

40% ABV	MOLASSES	DOUBLE COLUMN STILL	THE HELIOS DISTILLERY

FLAVOUR

The Helios Distillery, located in Okinawa, Japan, has a rich history dating back to its founding in 1961. In 1981, the distillery expanded and started producing rum, making it one of the first rum producers in Japan.

Kiyomi, which means "pure beauty", is made from local molasses that is fermented for more than three weeks, distilled, and then rested in stainless steel. The rum offers aromas of savoury cucumber, overripened sugarcane, and brine, which continue on the palate alongside citrus peel.

OLD MONK 7-YEAR-OLD VATTED RUM

42.8% ABV	MOLASSES	TRADITIONAL POT STILL	KASAULI DISTILLERY

FLAVOUR

Launched in 1954, Old Monk Rum is an iconic Indian dark rum distilled at the Kasauli Distillery in Himachal Pradesh. Blended in vats for a minimum of seven years, this rum has dark caramel colouring made from sugar, which is traditional in rum making when creating a dark expression for market.

It has warm aromas of molasses, vanilla, caramel, caramelized sugar, and hints of oak. The palate offers toffee and butterscotch, with hints of spice and more soft wood, and a bitter sweetness on the finish.

RYOMA JAPANESE RUM 7 YEARS

40% ABV	SUGARCANE JUICE	POT STILL	KIKUSUI DISTILLERY

FLAVOUR

The Kikusui Distillery, located on the island of Shikoku, Japan, is generally known for making saké. It also crafts rum from pressed sugarcane grown on the oldest farm in Japan.

This seven-year-old rum is matured in old Japanese oak barrels, some of which previously held saké, to mellow the rum. It has tropical aromas of mango, passion fruit, and honeysuckle. On the palate, there is vanilla, brown sugar, and oak, with a long, sweet finish of spicy ginger.

TANDUAY DOUBLE RUM

40% ABV	MOLASSES	MULTI-COLUMN STILL	TANDUAY DISTILLERS, INC.

FLAVOUR

With a history that dates back to 1854, Tanduay is officially the world's biggest-selling rum brand, although most of it is consumed in the Philippines, where it is made.

This sweet, fruity rum is produced by blending 16-year-old and five-year-old rums, then marrying them in ex-bourbon casks for another two years. The older rum mellows the younger one in the barrel, creating flavours of caramel, cooked pineapple, and almonds, with dried fruits and nuts and a light, woody finish on the tongue.

AFRICA

Africa boasts a rich and varied connection to the alcohol market, spanning centuries of tradition and innovation. It embraces ancient beer-brewing practices dating back thousands of years, and the cultivation of sugarcane for rum production.

WHAT MAKES AFRICAN RUM UNIQUE?

Although there are no fewer than 54 African countries, and more than half of them grow sugarcane, Africa's rum industry has yet to fulfil its potential. But the future is bright, as rum brands embrace the rich landscape of Africa to craft world-class rums.

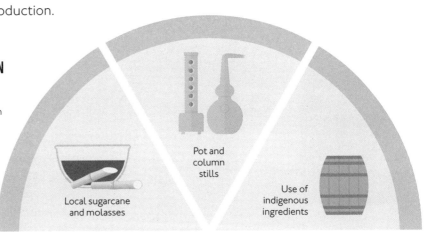

Local sugarcane and molasses

Pot and column stills

Use of indigenous ingredients

TYPES OF AFRICAN RUM

There are many countries within the continent that have used their African heritage, know-how, and ex-colonial trade links to venture onto the international rum market. Mauritius, for instance, makes rums from both molasses and sugarcane juice that are popular in France and the UK. South African rums like MHOBA are seeing success in the craft rum arena, as connoisseurs seek out the high-ester, funky style associated with the distillery. Rum from the Seychelles is also growing in stature, as the islands not only make their own style from both pot and column stills, but also are marrying imported rum from the Caribbean to recreate an "African Caribbean" connection in their blends. Africa's diverse climates and landscapes have given rise to a wide array of indigenous ingredients used in many rums, such as Ghanaian brand Reign, which is ageing rum in ex-cashew apple brandy barrels made from local wood.

MIXERS

OLD JAMAICA Ginger Beer
THE LONDON ESSENCE Roasted Pineapple Crafted Soda
FEVER-TREE Spiced Orange Ginger Ale

COCKTAILS

JUNGLE BIRD see pp200–01
MAI TAI see pp203–04
RUM PUNCH see pp212–13

OTHER RUMS TO TRY

ELIZABETH YARD SAVANNA (Réunion)
BAHARI BLUE (Kenya)
OAKS & ÂMES VSOP (Mauritius)

CHAMAREL PREMIUM XO

| 43% ABV | SUGARCANE JUICE | POT STILL | LA RHUMERIE DE CHAMAREL |

FLAVOUR

SWEET · SPICY · WOODY · HERBAL · RICH · FRUITY

The Chamarel Distillery (La Rhumerie de Chamarel) was founded in 2008 on the island of Mauritius, and is known for its craft rum using sugarcane grown on the estate.

This XO, meaning "Extra Old", is a six-year-old, copper pot-stilled blend. It is aged in new and old French oak barrels at ageing facilities in the southeast of the island. This medium-dry rum has a flavour profile of stone fruit, dried grass, sugarcane, vanilla, sandalwood, and sweet spices.

DZAMA CUVÉE NOIRE PRESTIGE

| 40% ABV | MOLASSES | COLUMN STILL | VIDZAR CO. |

FLAVOUR

SWEET · SPICY · WOODY · HERBAL · RICH · FRUITY

Dzama Rum was founded in 1981 on the island of Nosy Be, off the northwest coast of Madagascar, with production moving to the capital, Antananarivo, in 1984.

The sweet-tasting Dzama Cuvée Noire Prestige is a blend of rums from Ambilobe and Namakia, two distilleries located in the north of Madagascar. The molasses used to make the rum comes from local sugarcane that grows alongside spices. These spices are found in the rum's profile, such as vanilla, cloves, and pepper, as well as ylang-ylang.

MHOBA FRENCH CASK SELECT RESERVE

65% ABV	SUGARCANE JUICE	STAINLESS STEEL POT STILL	MHOBA DISTILLERY

FLAVOUR

SWEET · SPICY · WOODY · HERBAL · RICH · FRUITY

If you're ever in the hills of the Onderberg district of Mpumalanga, you'll find the MHOBA Distillery, in Malalane, making authentic artisanal South African rum.

Made from local pressed sugarcane, the juice is fermented, batched distilled, and then aged for more than two years in ex-Cape red wine casks made from French oak. The rum displays notes of oak, shaved wood, dried fruit, and spices, with a warm palate of tropical fruit, leather, sugarcane, oak, and more spices.

NEW GROVE EMOTION 1969

47% ABV	MOLASSES	TRADITIONAL COLUMN STILL	GRAYS DISTILLERY

FLAVOUR

SWEET · SPICY · WOODY · HERBAL · RICH · FRUITY

Created entirely from grass to glass at the distillery, single estate New Grove rums have quickly become one of the benchmarks for the Mauritius spirits industry. This unique rum is blend of vintages from 1969 to 2008, and is predominantly aged in old whisky barrels.

On the nose there are aromas of vanilla, tropical and citrus fruit, spice, and caramel. The palate brings warm molasses, nutmeg, allspice, and a touch of dusty oak, with a long finish of more oak, sweet spices, and dark chocolate.

REIGN AGED RUM

50% ABV	SUGARCANE JUICE	POT STILL	REIGNFOREST DISTILLERY

FLAVOUR

The ReignForest Distillery, formerly the Mim Distillery, is nestled on the border between Ghana's tropical rainforest and savannah. Its rum is crafted from local, organic sugarcane, which is pressed, fermented, and double distilled in purpose-built pot stills. It is then aged in new American oak barrels and ex-cashew apple brandy casks, which are married to create the final blend.

This light-bodied rum boasts subtle flavours of tropical fruits, with touches of nutty caramel, vanilla, sugarcane, red peppers, citrus, and cedarwood.

TAKAMAKA OVERPROOF RUM

69% ABV	MOLASSES	POT & COLUMN STILL	TROIS FRÈRES DISTILLERY

FLAVOUR

The Trois Frères Distillery on Mahé, the largest island of the Seychelles, opened its doors in 2002 to make pot-stilled rum from the local sugarcane. In 2020, the distillery expanded by introducing a column still, which is used to make rum from imported molasses, such as its overproof rum.

At a powerful 69% ABV, this rum delivers aromas and flavour of citrus, vanilla ice cream, and touches of banana, followed by tropical fruits and white pepper on the finish.

DEPENDENT BOTTLERS

Most rum brands don't have their own distillery, so some buy rum from a blending house, while others buy directly from a distillery to create their own unique blends.

WHAT MAKES DEPENDENT BOTTLERS' RUM UNIQUE?

Uniqueness is down to the bottlers' recipe and the style of rum they want to sell. They still have to abide by the laws of the region they sell into, such as the European Union (EU) or the US, but they do not have to adhere to the rules of the country in which the rum is made.

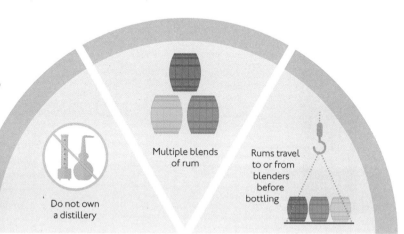

Do not own a distillery

Multiple blends of rum

Rums travel to or from blenders before bottling

TYPES OF INTERNATIONAL RUM

There many styles of blended rums, where several regions' rums are used to make or market the dependent bottlers' brands. Some rum companies are based in one territory but will blend and bottle in another. Pusser's Rum, from the British Virgin Islands, for instance is aged, blended, and bottled in Guyana. Equiano and Veritas are a blend of Mauritian and Jamaican rums, respectively, imported into Barbados and blended with local aged rums at the Foursquare Distillery. Spanish spirit maker Williams & Humbert imports Guyanese and Barbadian rums to Jerez to blend in its sherry casks to create Dos Maderas PX. Blackwell is a dependent Jamaican rum brand that is made by J. Wray & Nephew, who also make Appleton Estate rums. To make its famous Black Seal, Goslings buys rums from various distilleries and ages and blends locally in Bermuda, as there are no rum distilleries on the island.

MIXERS	COCKTAILS	OTHER RUMS TO TRY
THE LONDON ESSENCE Pink Grapefruit Crafted Soda	**DAIQUIRI** see pp194–95	**OLD ROAD RUM** (St Kitts)
FRANKLIN & SONS Pineapple & Almond Soda	**MAI TAI** see pp202–03	**HABITATION VELIER** (Italy)
FEVER-TREE Spiced Orange Ginger Ale	**RUM MANHATTAN**	**DUPPY SHARE XO** (England)

BLACK TOT MASTER BLENDER'S RESERVE 2024 EDITION

54.5% ABV	MOLASSES	POT & COLUMN STILL	ELIXIR DISTILLERS LTD

FLAVOUR

SWEET · SPICY · WOODY · HERBAL · RICH · FRUITY

The Black Tot Master Blender's Reserve is an annual bottling commemorating Black Tot Day on 31 July 1970. On that day, the Royal Navy officially ended its centuries-old tradition of providing sailors with a daily rum ration, known as a "tot".

The recipe for this particular rum changes every year, and the 2024 edition uses rums from Jamaica, Trinidad, Barbados, and Guyana. It has rich aromas of banoffee pie, butterscotch, and sweet oak, with a big palate of spicy cherry, cinnamon, allspice, nutmeg, cocoa, and caramel.

DOS MADERAS 5+5 PX

40% ABV	MOLASSES	POT & COLUMN STILL	BODEGAS WILLIAMS & HUMBERT

FLAVOUR

SWEET · SPICY · WOODY · HERBAL · RICH · FRUITY

Dos Maderas, which means "two woods", begins its journey in Barbados and Guyana, where the rums are aged for five years in American oak barrels. Both rums then travel to Spain, where they are transferred to sherry casks in a *solera* system (see p87) for another three years. Finally, the eight-year-old rum is added to Pedro Ximenez sherry casks in a *solera* system for two more years.

The result is a rum with rich caramel, dried fruits, hints of spice, PX sherry, and chocolate, with a lingering sweetness.

EQUIANO ORIGINAL DARK

43% ABV	MOLASSES	DOUBLE RETORT POT & TRADITIONAL COLUMN	FOURSQUARE DISTILLERY & EQUIANO RUM CO. LTD

FLAVOUR

SWEET · SPICY · WOODY · HERBAL · RICH · FRUITY

Equiano Rum is the world's first African and Caribbean rum blend and a marriage of two rums. The first is a Mauritian molasses-based rum aged for 10 years in ex-Cognac barrels. The second is a Barbadian molasses-based rum aged for eight years in ex-bourbon barrels.

The finished rum has rich notes of dried fruits such as raisins and sultanas combined with sweet toffee, butterscotch, and caramel. It finishes with a suggestion of orange peel, vanilla, and buttered wood.

GOSLINGS BLACK SEAL

40% ABV	MOLASSES	POT & COLUMN STILL	GOSLINGS BROTHERS LTD

FLAVOUR

SWEET · SPICY · WOODY · HERBAL · RICH · FRUITY

In the sunny embrace of Bermuda's shores, amid the rhythmic sway of palm trees and waves, lies the illustrious tale of Goslings Rum. The black seal on the label represents the black wax seal that kept old bottles of rum airtight in the past.

The dark spirit, the main component of the iconic Dark 'n' Stormy cocktail (see pp208–09), is a selection of Caribbean rums that have been aged and blended. It has flavours of banana, sticky toffee, chocolate, treacle, and molasses on the palate.

PUSSER'S GUNPOWDER PROOF

| 54.5% ABV | MOLASSES | POT & COLUMN STILL | DIAMOND DISTILLERY & PUSSER'S RUM LTD |

FLAVOUR

Pusser's Gunpowder Proof is based on the style of rum that the Royal Navy produced in accordance with the Admiralty's blending recipe. It was last used when the Royal Navy discontinued its daily ration on 31 July 1970, known as Black Tot Day.

Bottled at navy strength (54.5% ABV), it has rich aromas of treacle, caramel, molasses, honey, vanilla, and a touch of cinnamon, followed by sugarcane honey, stone fruit, and more caramel, with nutmeg, ginger spice, and light oak on the finish. Perfect in a Painkiller (see pp196–97).

VERITAS

| 47% ABV | MOLASSES | DOUBLE RETORT POT & COFFEY COLUMN | FOURSQUARE DISTILLERY & VELIER |

FLAVOUR

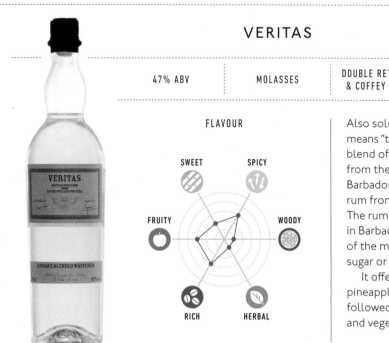

Also sold as Probitas, Veritas, which means "truth" in Latin, is a harmonious blend of traditional Coffey still rum from the Foursquare Distillery in Barbados and a two-year-old pot still rum from Jamaica's Hampden Estate. The rums are blended and bottled in Barbados under the watchful eyes of the master blender, who adds no sugar or spices to the rum.

It offers aromas of creamy vanilla, pineapple, and fresh sugarcane, followed by lime peel, molasses, and vegetal and white pepper notes.

CLASSIC
---- RUM ----
COCKTAILS

RUM COCKTAILS HAVE played a significant role in the rich history of rum, showcasing the spirit's versatility and cultural impact. The Rum Punch reflects tropical simplicity, combining rum with local ingredients such as lime, sugar, water, and spice. The Piña Colada, born in Puerto Rico and now its national cocktail, celebrates the tropical essence of rum with coconut cream and pineapple juice. The Daiquiri, like so many classics originating in Cuba, highlights the simple trinity of rum, lime, and sugar. These cocktails not only demonstrate the diverse flavour profiles of rum but also provide a connection to the traditions and stories of the regions where rum has historical significance. They can transport drinkers to a tropical location, and all for the price of a drink.

COCKTAIL-MAKING EQUIPMENT

Making rum cocktails is almost as good as drinking them. With many styles of classic drinks to make, it's always good to have a set of cocktail equipment at the ready, as you never know when an impromptu rum cocktail party might start.

COCKTAIL SHAKER

The cocktail shaker allows you to thoroughly mix ingredients and chill them properly. It comes in various styles, such as the classic three-piece cobbler shaker and the two-piece Boston shaker. The shaker base can also double up as a mixing vessel to stir cocktails with ice before straining them into a glass.

JIGGER

Precision is key in cocktail making, and a jigger ensures accurate measurements of ingredients. Typically featuring two different-sized cups, such as 15ml/30ml (½fl oz/1 fl oz), a jigger allows you to maintain consistency in your cocktails, ensuring a perfect balance of flavours.

BAR SPOON

Often underestimated but incredibly versatile, a bar spoon is essential for gentle stirring and layering ingredients. Its long handle makes it ideal for reaching the bottom of mixing glasses and creating beautiful, layered drinks. Some spoons have a flat handle end, which can be used as a small muddler.

MUDDLER

For cocktails that require muddled, or bruised, ingredients, such as a classic Mojito (see pp206–07) or a Caipirinha, a muddler is indispensable. Use it to gently crush fruits, herbs, or sugar cubes to release their flavours or essential oils, adding depth and complexity to your cocktails.

STRAINER

A strainer is essential for removing ice, fruit pulp, or other solid ingredients when pouring the drink into a glass. They include the Hawthorne strainer and the fine-mesh or tea strainer, both ensuring a flawless pour. Julep strainers are handy when making drinks in a mixing glass with large ice cubes.

CITRUS JUICER

Fresh citrus juice is a cornerstone of many rum cocktails. A juicer allows you to extract juice from lemons, limes, and other citrus fruits quickly and efficiently. Manual juicers used by bartenders are usually a two-handled hinged device known as a Mexican elbow, but you can use any domestic juicer.

BLENDER

A blender is indispensable for creating frozen or slushy drinks like a Piña Colada (see pp210–11). It efficiently blends ice, rum, fruits, and other ingredients into creamy and refreshing drinks. Some tropical drinks call for a "flash blend", which means blending for two or three seconds to create the perfect consistency.

MIXING GLASS

A mixing glass is a staple when making craft cocktails. The clear glass allows visual assessment, promoting controlled dilution and temperature regulation. It is essential for classics like a Rum Manhattan and stirred drinks, and embodies elegance and expertise in mixology.

SIMPLE SYRUP

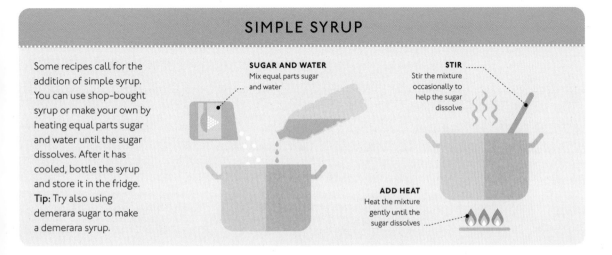

Some recipes call for the addition of simple syrup. You can use shop-bought syrup or make your own by heating equal parts sugar and water until the sugar dissolves. After it has cooled, bottle the syrup and store it in the fridge. **Tip:** Try also using demerara sugar to make a demerara syrup.

SUGAR AND WATER
Mix equal parts sugar and water

STIR
Stir the mixture occasionally to help the sugar dissolve

ADD HEAT
Heat the mixture gently until the sugar dissolves

CUBA LIBRE

Rum, cola, and a little lime is probably the most common way to drink rum, and this highball is a staple in any bar that serves rum. The Cuba Libre, born amid the effervescence of Havana after the Spanish-American War (1898), is a timeless cocktail that embodies the spirit of liberation and celebration.

HISTORY

The Cuba Libre, Spanish for "free Cuba", traces its origins to Havana in the late 1890s. Legend has it that American soldiers, celebrating the newfound liberty of Cuba, mixed local rum with cola and a squeeze of lime, creating the iconic cocktail. Some historians claim that Coca Cola was only introduced into Cuba during the early 1900s, so the original Cuba Libre may have been La Canchánchara, a cocktail of Cuban rum, lime, and brown sugar or molasses. However, the cola version soared in popularity on the island as cola became more available, and, coupled with an increase in American trade and tourism, it became a symbol of camaraderie and shared freedom.

WHAT MAKES A CUBA LIBRE?

Fill a highball glass with plenty of ice. Pour in a generous amount of Cuban or light rum (a double shot if you're measuring), squeeze in the juice of half a lime, and top with cola. Stir gently. Garnish with a lime wedge or reuse the squeezed lime shell as a garnish.

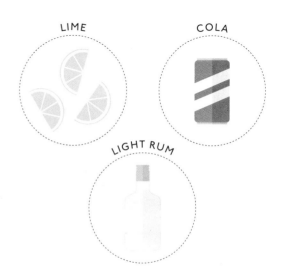

LIME

COLA

LIGHT RUM

THE CUBA LIBRE THROUGH TIME

1898

American soldiers call La Canchánchara, a local drink of rum, molasses, and lime, a Cuba Libre.

EARLY 1900s

Coca Cola is introduced to Cuba, replacing the sugar in the new version of the cocktail.

1920s

Highball cocktails such as the Cuba Libre continue to be popular with American tourists in Cuba during the US Prohibition era.

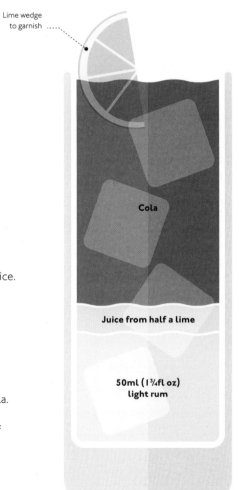

Lime wedge to garnish

Cola

Juice from half a lime

50ml (1¾fl oz)
light rum

METHOD

1. Fill a highball glass with ice.

2. Pour in 50ml (1¾fl oz) light rum.

3. Add the juice from half a lime.

4. Top up the glass with cola.

5. Garnish with a wedge of lime or the lime shell.

WHICH RUM?

HAVANA CLUB AÑEJO 7 AÑOS

EMINENTE RESERVA 7

SAOCAN RESERVA
ORIGINAL 10

DURING PROHIBITION IN THE UNITED STATES, AMERICANS FLOCKED TO CUBA, AND THE POPULARITY OF THE CUBA LIBRE SOARED.

DAIQUIRI

There is no more refreshing cocktail than a well-made Daiquiri. Pronounced *dai–ki–ri*, it simply combines a "tropical trinity" of rum, lime, and sugar. Easy. The Daiquiri is also one of the few classic cocktails where we have written proof of the creator and the original recipe.

HISTORY

The Daiquiri, a Cuban classic, traces its roots to the Spanish-American War (1898). American engineer Jennings Stockton Cox improvised a refreshing cocktail in the Cuban mining town of Daiquirí using local ingredients – rum, limes, sugar, and ice. This simple concoction evolved at Havana's El Floridita bar, where skilled bartenders like Constantino Ribalaigua Vert refined it, introducing variations of the house Daiquiri and the famous Hemingway Special, also known as the Papa Doble. The cocktail's popularity transcended borders, becoming a global favourite in the 20th century. Known for its versatility, the Daiquiri endures as a timeless drink, cherished for its elegance and historical significance.

WHAT MAKES A DAIQUIRI?

To make a classic Daiquiri, combine two parts of white rum, one part of fresh lime juice, and a half part of simple syrup in a shaker with ice. Shake well, then strain into a chilled cocktail glass. Garnish with a lime wheel or twist of lime, or serve without a garnish.

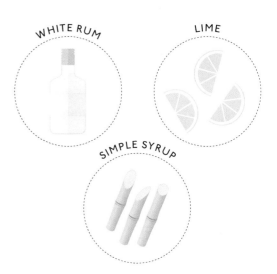

WHITE RUM

LIME

SIMPLE SYRUP

THE DAIQUIRI THROUGH TIME

1898

The original recipe is handwritten by Jennings Stockton Cox, an American working for the Spanish-American Iron Company.

1909

US Admiral Lucius Johnson visits Cox in Cuba and takes the Daiquiri recipe back to the Army & Navy Club in Washington, DC.

1931

Bartender Constantino Ribalaigua Vert of El Floridita in Havana popularizes the Frozen Daiquiri, using shaved ice and an electric blender.

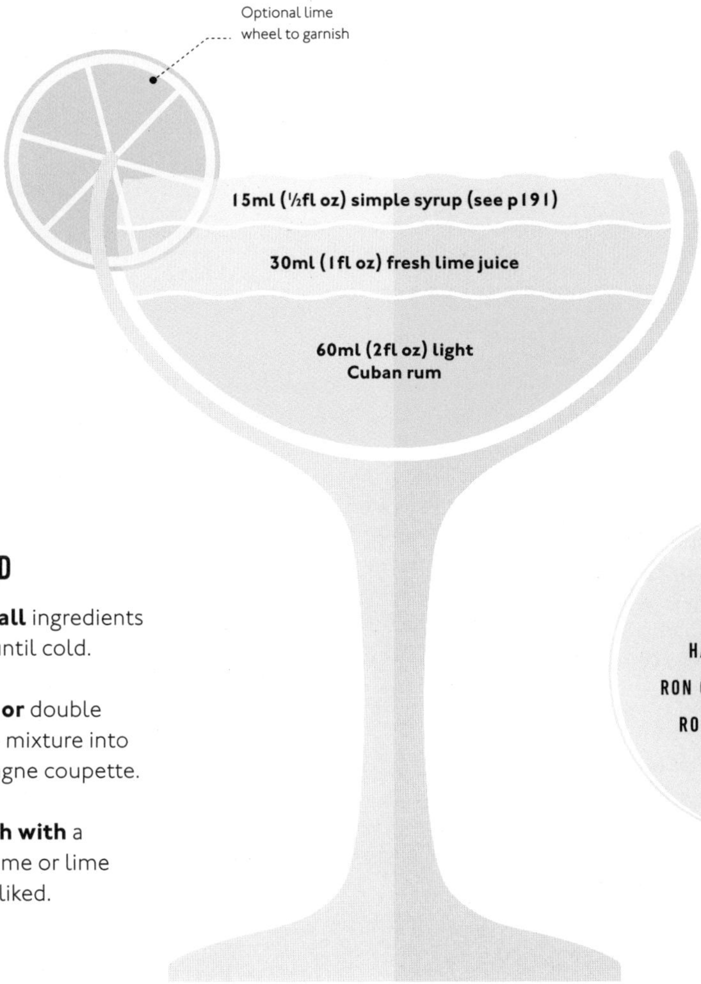

Optional lime
wheel to garnish

15ml (½fl oz) simple syrup (see p191)

30ml (1fl oz) fresh lime juice

60ml (2fl oz) light
Cuban rum

METHOD

1. Shake all ingredients
with ice until cold.

2. Single or double
strain the mixture into
a champagne coupette.

3. Garnish with a
twist of lime or lime
wheel, if liked.

WHICH RUM?

**HAVANA CLUB 3 AÑOS
RON CUBAY 3 CARTA BLANCA
RON SANTIAGO DE CUBA
CARTA BLANCA**

"MY MOJITO IN LA BODEGUITA,
MY DAIQUIRI IN EL FLORIDITA" –
ERNEST HEMINGWAY.

DARK 'N' STORMY

The Dark 'n' Stormy, a captivating cocktail born in Bermuda, merges the rich flavour of dark rum with the zing of ginger beer. Its deep, amber hues mirror the tempestuous sea, while the effervescence and warmth evoke the spirit of the Caribbean. A true classic, it's a sip of tropical spice.

HISTORY

The Dark 'n' Stormy cocktail, a maritime classic, traces its roots to the island of Bermuda. In the early 20th century, British naval officers mixed Goslings Black Seal Rum with ginger beer, creating a bold and effervescent concoction. It quickly became a local favourite, and almost a century later, it is the most popular cocktail on the island and is known as Bermuda's national cocktail. The name, reminiscent of Bermuda's stormy seas, emerged from its visual resemblance to a tempest. Goslings Rum trademarked the term "Dark 'n' Stormy", asserting that its Black Seal Rum is crucial for authenticity. The drink's popularity transcended Bermuda, becoming a symbol of seafaring culture and also a favourite at yachting events.

WHAT MAKES A DARK 'N' STORMY?

To many bars around the world, a Dark 'n' Stormy basically means any dark rum, ginger beer, and a wedge of lime. This popular highball should also have plenty of ice. It is a great, simple serve for all seasons and a refreshing alternative to a Rum and Coke.

GINGER BEER

LIME WEDGE

DARK RUM

THE DARK 'N' STORMY THROUGH TIME

EARLY 20TH CENTURY

The Dark 'n' Stormy is believed to have originated in Bermuda, with British naval officers mixing Goslings Black Seal Rum and ginger beer.

AFTER 1918

The cocktail gains favour in Bermuda and among sailors, becoming a maritime classic.

1980

Goslings Rum officially trademarks the name "Dark 'n' Stormy" in Bermuda.

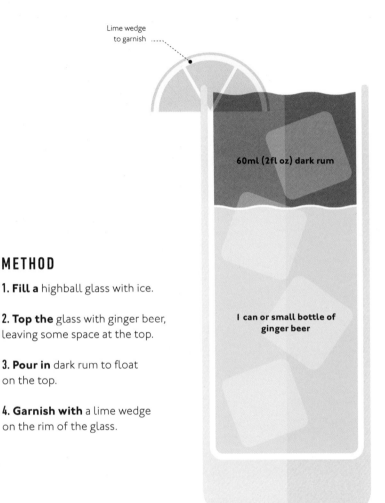

Lime wedge
to garnish

60ml (2fl oz) dark rum

I can or small bottle of
ginger beer

METHOD

1. Fill a highball glass with ice.

2. Top the glass with ginger beer,
leaving some space at the top.

3. Pour in dark rum to float
on the top.

4. Garnish with a lime wedge
on the rim of the glass.

WHICH RUM?

GOSLINGS BLACK SEAL

SKIPPER FINE OLD
DEMERARA

MOUNT GAY BLACK
BARREL

ONE STORY ALLEGES THAT THE DARK 'N'
STORMY GOT ITS NAME BECAUSE IT IS
"THE COLOUR OF A CLOUD ONLY A FOOL
OR A DEAD MAN WOULD SAIL UNDER".

THE HURRICANE

Thought to have originated in 1939 at the Hurricane Bar, New York City, this passion fruit and rum cocktail was undoubtedly made famous at Pat O'Brien's in New Orleans. While the famous drink was said to have been created out of necessity, the Hurricane cocktail has endured as a symbol of New Orleans' vibrant cocktail culture.

HISTORY

Originally, the Hurricane was created as a solution to surplus rum. During World War II (1939–45), US distributors required bars to purchase multiple cases of less popular rum to get a case of more desirable spirits, like whiskey. To manage this surplus, Pat O'Brien concocted a fruity and potent cocktail, served in large glasses shaped like hurricane lamps, which became the cocktail's namesake. The initial recipe typically included light and dark rum, passion fruit juice, lime juice, and simple syrup. Over the years, variations emerged, with the most famous recipe incorporating grenadine or orange juice. The cocktail gained popularity and is still today a signature drink associated with New Orleans.

WHAT MAKES A HURRICANE?

This boozy rum cocktail is best served ice cold and in a hurricane glass or *poco grande* (piña colada glass). Try to use fresh passion fruit and orange juice for texture, and a sweet, bright red grenadine syrup for the cocktail's iconic red hue.

RUM

PASSION FRUIT JUICE

ORANGE JUICE

LIME JUICE

GRENADINE SYRUP

THE HURRICANE THROUGH TIME

1939

Stories emerge of a Hurricane cocktail being served in New York during the 1939 World's Fair.

1940s

The Hurricane cocktail is officially born at Pat O'Brien's Bar in New Orleans, using surplus rum in a fruity concoction.

1970s–1980s

The drink gains widespread popularity, becoming a signature New Orleans cocktail, especially on iconic Bourbon Street.

Orange wheel
and cherry to
garnish

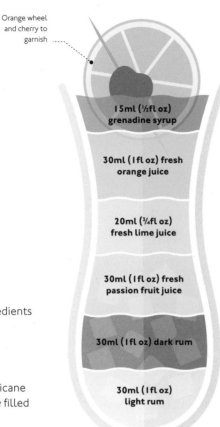

15ml (½fl oz)
grenadine syrup

30ml (1fl oz) fresh
orange juice

20ml (¾fl oz)
fresh lime juice

30ml (1fl oz) fresh
passion fruit juice

30ml (1fl oz) dark rum

30ml (1fl oz)
light rum

METHOD

1. Place all the ingredients in a shaker with ice.

2. Shake until cold.

3. Strain into a hurricane glass or *poco grande* filled with ice.

4. Garnish with an orange wheel and a cherry.

WHICH RUM?

BAYOU RESERVE

ROULAISON TRADITIONAL
POT DISTILLED RUM

OLD NEW ORLEANS
AMBER RUM

A HURRICANE GLASS HAS A SIMILAR
SHAPE TO A *POCO GRANDE*, BUT IS
TALLER AND MUCH BIGGER.

JUNGLE BIRD

In the tropical drinks world, there are very few cocktail recipes that call for the bittersweet taste of Campari, an Italian aperitif that is ever present in all the upscale bars, and it's rarely mixed or associated with tropical flavours. But the Jungle Bird is one of those drinks.

HISTORY

The Jungle Bird, a vibrant and exotic creation, emerged in 1973 at the Kuala Lumpur Hilton, in Malaysia, as the welcome drink for the hotel's opening. Crafted by beverage manager Jeffrey Ong at the Aviary Bar, this tiki-style libation marries the richness of a dark rum with the bittersweet allure of Campari and the tropical sweetness of pineapple juice, delivering a unique and unforgettable flavour experience. The drink is said to have been originally served in a ceramic bird vessel and sipped from an opening in the tail. In recent years, the Jungle Bird has gained popularity in the cocktail scene, and when made well, is celebrated for its balance of sweetness, bitterness, and richness.

WHAT MAKES A JUNGLE BIRD?

For the perfect Jungle Bird, shake dark rum, Campari, simple syrup, pineapple juice, and fresh lime juice with ice. Strain into a tiki mug or highball glass over ice. Garnish with pineapple leaves or a wedge of pineapple. This balance of bold flavours creates a bittersweet, fruity cocktail.

LIME JUICE

SIMPLE SYRUP

PINEAPPLE JUICE

CAMPARI

DARK RUM

THE JUNGLE BIRD THROUGH TIME

1973

Jeffrey Ong, beverage manager at the Kuala Lumpur Hilton, crafts the Jungle Bird as the hotel's opening welcome drink.

1989

A recipe for the Jungle Bird appears in John J. Poister's *New American Bartender's Guide*.

1990s ONWARDS

Over the years, the cocktail transcends its origin, becoming a cherished classic in the international cocktail scene.

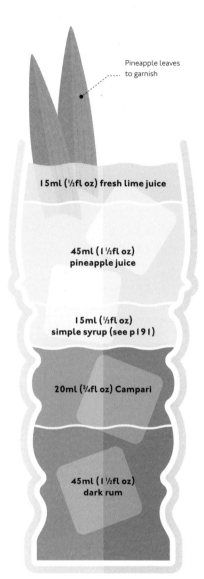

Pineapple leaves to garnish

15ml (½fl oz) fresh lime juice

45ml (1½fl oz) pineapple juice

15ml (½fl oz) simple syrup (see p191)

20ml (¾fl oz) Campari

45ml (1½fl oz) dark rum

METHOD

1. Add all the ingredients to a shaker with ice.

2. Shake well to chill the mixture.

3. Strain into a tiki mug or highball glass filled with ice.

4. Garnish with pineapple leaves or a wedge of pineapple.

WHICH RUM?

OLD MONK 7 YEAR OLD

TANDUAY DOUBLE RUM

APPLETON ESTATE
8 YEAR OLD RESERVE

WITH ITS BLEND OF RUM, CAMPARI, AND TROPICAL FRUIT JUICES, THE JUNGLE BIRD GAINED PROMINENCE IN THE TIKI COCKTAIL CULTURE.

MAI TAI

If there is one cocktail that epitomizes the tropical cocktail genre, then it would be the Mai Tai. This tropical elixir, with roots in the exoticism of mid-20th-century tiki culture, is a Polynesian-inspired cocktail that embodies the spirit of paradise in a glass.

HISTORY

The Mai Tai has a contested but captivating history. Widely credited to American bartender and entrepreneur Victor "Trader Vic" Bergeron in the 1940s, the cocktail was a blend of a 17-year-old Jamaican rum, lime juice, orange liqueur, sugar, and orgeat syrup. Its name allegedly came about in response to guests proclaiming *"Maita'i roa a'e!"*, meaning "Out of this world!" in Tahitian, when tasting the cocktail for the first time. The Mai Tai gained popularity as an exotic and sophisticated libation, becoming a symbol of Polynesian escapism.

WHAT MAKES A MAI TAI?

The aged rum forms the base, providing depth and complexity. Freshly squeezed lime juice contributes brightness and acidity. Orange liqueur, such as orange curaçao or triple sec, adds citrus sweetness to enhance the rum's citrus notes, while the orgeat syrup imparts almond undertones to complement any nuttiness from the heavy rum.

LIME JUICE

SIMPLE SYRUP

HEAVY AGED RUM

ORGEAT SYRUP

ORANGE CURAÇAO

THE MAI TAI THROUGH TIME

1933

American businessman Donn Beach creates a cocktail called the Q.B. Cooler. Years later, it is assumed to be the inspiration for Trader Vic's Mai Tai.

1944

Trader Vic claims to invent the Mai Tai at his Oakland restaurant in California, in the United States.

2023

Rum company J. Wray & Nephew launches a limited edition 17-year-old rum called The Legend, so bartenders can recreate the 1944 recipe using a similar rum.

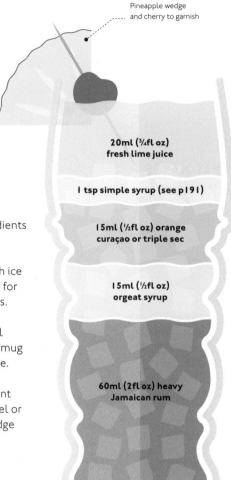

Pineapple wedge and cherry to garnish

20ml (¾fl oz) fresh lime juice

1 tsp simple syrup (see p191)

15ml (½fl oz) orange curaçao or triple sec

15ml (½fl oz) orgeat syrup

60ml (2fl oz) heavy Jamaican rum

METHOD

1. Pour all the ingredients into a shaker.

2. Fill the shaker with ice and shake vigorously for about 10–15 seconds.

3. Strain the cocktail into a tiki or tropical mug over fresh crushed ice.

4. Garnish with a mint sprig and a lime wheel or with a pineapple wedge and a cherry.

WHICH RUM?

APPLETON ESTATE
12 YEAR OLD RARE CASKS

WORTHY PARK 109

EL DORADO
15 YEAR OLD

"MAITA'I ROA A'E" ROUGHLY TRANSLATES AS "VERY GOOD" OR "OUT OF THIS WORLD".

MARY PICKFORD

Named after one of the most powerful women in the film industry during the 1920s, the Mary Pickford is a fruitily sweet, tangy, tropical cocktail that became one of the most popular drinks during a time when Americans flocked to Cuba to escape Prohibition.

HISTORY

The Mary Pickford was created in the 1920s by Fred Kaufman at the Hotel Nacional de Cuba (some say it was another barman named Eddie Woelke) in honour of Mary Pickford, the silent movie star and co-founder of United Artists film studio. Pickford may or may not have visited Cuba prior to the drink's invention, but a story about the drink was retold by Basil Woon in his 1928 book *When It's Cocktail Time in Cuba*: "The Mary Pickford… is two-thirds pineapple-juice and one-third Bacardí, with a dash of grenadine. The pineapple juice must be fresh-squeezed." Later recipes called for a dash of maraschino liqueur, which is now seen as an essential ingredient.

WHAT MAKES A MARY PICKFORD?

The key to a great-tasting Mary Pickford is the tanginess of the freshly squeezed pineapple juice. If you only have concentrated pineapple juice, then add a spoonful of lime juice to balance the flavours of this tropical drink.

PINEAPPLE JUICE

GRENADINE

MARASCHINO LIQUEUR

LIGHT RUM

THE MARY PICKFORD THROUGH TIME

1920s

Two bartenders, Fred Kaufman and Eddie Woelke, both claim credit for the creation of this cocktail.

1928

The first-known recipe for the Mary Pickford cocktail appears in the 1928 book *When It's Cocktail Time in Cuba* by Basil Woon.

1930s

After the end of Prohibition in 1933, classic cocktails like the Mary Pickford continue to be enjoyed, although popularity fluctuates.

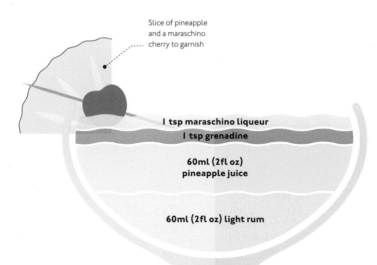

Slice of pineapple
and a maraschino
cherry to garnish

1 tsp maraschino liqueur

1 tsp grenadine

60ml (2fl oz)
pineapple juice

60ml (2fl oz) light rum

METHOD

1. Fill a cocktail shaker with ice.

2. Add all the ingredients to
the shaker.

3. Shake well until the ingredients
are chilled and combined.

4. Strain the mixture into a
chilled cocktail glass.

5. Garnish with a maraschino
cherry and a pineapple wedge.

WHICH RUM?

HAVANA CLUB 3 YEAR OLD

VERITAS

RON CUBAY 3 YEAR
CARTA BLANCA

THE PINEAPPLE JUICE MUST BE FRESHLY
SQUEEZED. IF NOT, THEN ADD A TOUCH
OF LIME JUICE FOR TANGINESS.

MOJITO

Sipping a Mojito is like taking a holiday in a glass – the cool breeze of mint, the sunshine burst of lime, and the smooth waves of rum transport us to the laidback charm of Cuba with every delightful sip. Over time, this refreshing Cuban cocktail has become a globally celebrated, iconic, and beloved summer drink.

HISTORY

The Mojito, a quintessential Cuban cocktail, has a history dating back centuries. Originating in the 16th century, it evolved from a medicinal concoction made by Indigenous Taíno people that combined sugarcane juice, lime, and mint. Over time, the drink absorbed influences from Spanish and African cultures. By the 19th century, it gained popularity in Havana. Its iconic form evolved with the addition of rum, soda water, and ice. The Mojito thrived, capturing the hearts of locals and visitors alike. In the 21st century, it experienced a global resurgence, achieving international fame as a refreshing, minty elixir. Today, the Cuban Mojito delights cocktail enthusiasts worldwide.

WHAT MAKES A MOJITO?

Lightly muddle fresh mint leaves and a spoonful of sugar in a glass. Add ice (cubed for the original way or crushed for the modern way), light rum, and the juice of one lime. Top with soda water, stirring gently. Garnish with mint leaves and a lime wedge.

LIME

SIMPLE SYRUP OR SUGAR

LIGHT RUM

MINT LEAVES

SODA WATER

THE MOJITO THROUGH TIME

16TH CENTURY

The Mojito's origins can be traced back to the 16th century, when Indigenous Taíno people in Cuba create a prototype using sugarcane juice, lime, and mint.

20TH CENTURY

During Prohibition (1920–33) in the United States, Americans flock to Cuba, especially Havana, where they indulge in cocktails, particularly Mojitos.

21ST CENTURY

The Mojito experiences a global resurgence, gaining international fame as a classic cocktail. It becomes synonymous with Cuban culture.

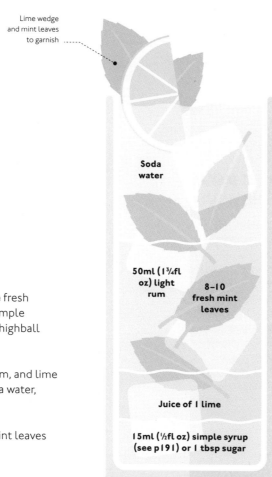

Lime wedge
and mint leaves
to garnish

Soda
water

50ml (1¾fl
oz) light
rum

8–10
fresh mint
leaves

Juice of 1 lime

15ml (½fl oz) simple syrup
(see p191) or 1 tbsp sugar

METHOD

1. Lightly muddle fresh mint leaves with simple syrup or sugar in a highball or Collins glass.

2. Add ice, light rum, and lime juice. Top with soda water, stirring gently.

3. Garnish with mint leaves and a lime wedge.

WHICH RUM?

HAVANA CLUB 3
BACARDÍ SUPERIOR
EQUIANO LIGHT

SIPPING A GOOD MOJITO IS LIKE TAKING
A HOLIDAY IN A GLASS, TRANSPORTING
YOU TO CUBA WITH EVERY SIP.

THE PAINKILLER

With its roots in the British Virgin Islands, the Painkiller is closely associated with the Soggy Dollar Bar on the island of Jost Van Dyke. The drink's creation is attributed to Daphne Henderson, the owner of the small beach bar, in the early 1970s, and it became famous with locals and visitors alike.

HISTORY

The Soggy Dollar Bar was so named because, when pulling up to the beautiful, white sandy beach by boat, the only way to get to the bar was to swim. And so patrons paid for their drinks with "soggy dollars". The original Painkiller recipe included imported dark rum, but legend has it that in the early 1980s, Charles Tobias, founder of locally produced Pusser's Navy Rum, persuaded the bar owner to tweak the recipe to include his unique dark rum. From then on, the Painkiller became synonymous not only with the island and bar but also the rum brand – so much so that Pusser's Rum filed a US trademark on the Painkiller's name and recipe in 1989.

WHAT MAKES A PAINKILLER?

Use a dark rum for an authentic flavour if you can't source Pusser's Rum. If you don't use freshly squeezed pineapple juice, then balance the sweetness of the drink with a touch of fresh lime juice. Be sure to use real cream of coconut such as Coco Reàl Infused Exotics.

DARK RUM

CREAM OF COCONUT

ORANGE JUICE

PINEAPPLE JUICE

NUTMEG

THE PAINKILLER THROUGH TIME

1970s

The iconic tropical cocktail is created at the Soggy Dollar Bar by owner Daphne Henderson.

MID-1980s

Entrepreneur Charles Tobias creates a new recipe for the cocktail using his Pusser's Navy Rum.

1989

Pusser's Rum Ltd files a US trademark on the Painkiller's name and recipe.

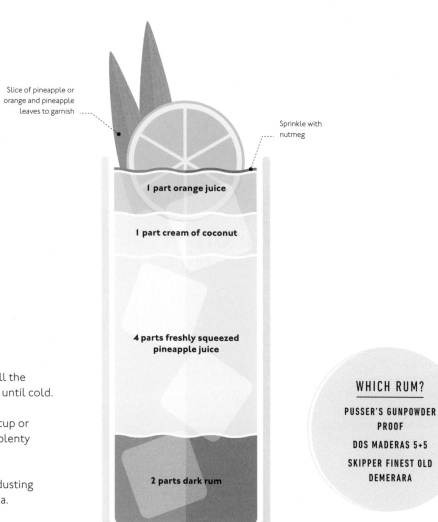

Slice of pineapple or orange and pineapple leaves to garnish

Sprinkle with nutmeg

1 part orange juice

1 part cream of coconut

4 parts freshly squeezed pineapple juice

2 parts dark rum

METHOD

1. Shake or blend all the ingredients with ice until cold.

2. Strain into a tin cup or highball glass with plenty of ice.

3. Sprinkle over a dusting of nutmeg for aroma.

4. Garnish with a slice of pineapple or orange and pineapple leaves.

WHICH RUM?

PUSSER'S GUNPOWDER PROOF

DOS MADERAS 5+5

SKIPPER FINEST OLD DEMERARA

THE PAINKILLER HAS BECOME SYNONYMOUS WITH PUSSER'S RUM, BUT ANY DARK RUM CAN BE USED.

PIÑA COLADA

In Spanish, the name "Piña Colada" translates as "strained pineapple", which refers to the freshly pressed and strained pineapple juice that should be used in the cocktail. Coupled with cream of coconut and a light rum, the drink is often associated with a tropical escape.

HISTORY

The Piña Colada has a story that originates in Old San Juan, Puerto Rico. The cocktail's modern creation is often credited to Ramón "Monchito" Marrero, a bartender at the Caribe Hilton in Old San Juan. In 1954, Monchito spent months experimenting with various ingredients, aiming to capture the essence of the island in a glass. His final concoction, the Piña Colada, became an instant hit with the hotel guests. Thanks to tourism, the cocktail's popularity soared globally, earning it the status of Puerto Rico's national drink. Today, the Piña Colada is synonymous with sandy beaches and the spirit of the Caribbean, making it a cherished classic in the world of tropical beverages.

WHAT MAKES A PIÑA COLADA?

To make a Piña Colada, blend light rum, pineapple juice, cream of coconut, and cream with ice until smooth. Pour the mixture into a chilled glass and garnish with a pineapple slice. Optionally, you can add a maraschino cherry and pineapple leaf for extra flair.

PINEAPPLE JUICE

CREAM OF COCONUT

LIGHT RUM

DOUBLE CREAM

THE PIÑA COLADA THROUGH TIME

DECEMBER 1922

Travel magazine includes what may be the first written reference to a drink named Piña Colada, although it does not contain coconut.

AUGUST 1954

Bartender Ramón "Monchito" Marrero is said to invent the modern-day recipe at the Caribe Hilton in Old San Juan, Puerto Rico.

1978

The Piña Colada is declared the official drink of Puerto Rico, solidifying its cultural significance.

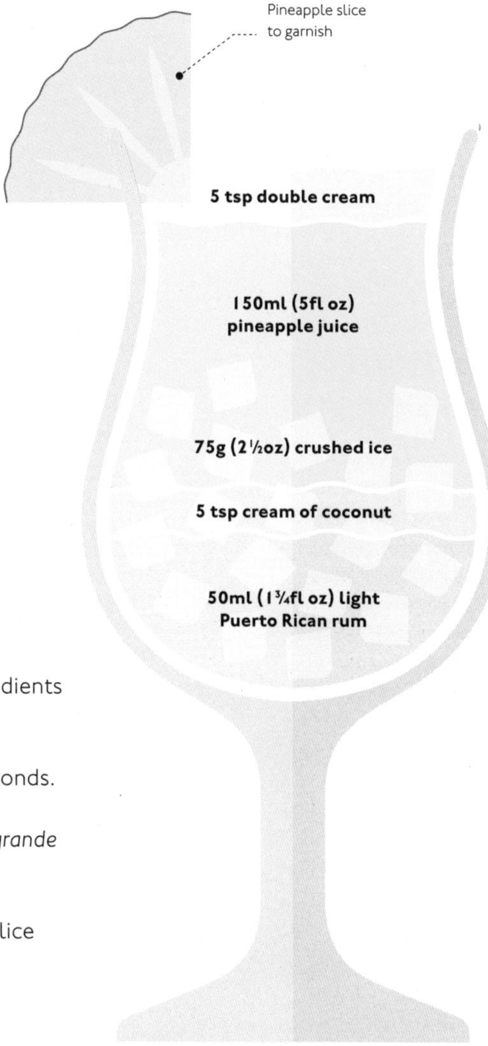

Pineapple slice
to garnish

5 tsp double cream

150ml (5fl oz)
pineapple juice

75g (2½oz) crushed ice

5 tsp cream of coconut

50ml (1¾fl oz) light
Puerto Rican rum

METHOD

1. Add all the ingredients
to a blender.

2. Blend for 15 seconds.

3. Serve in a *poco grande*
(piña colada) glass.

4. Garnish with a slice
of pineapple.

WHICH RUM?

DON Q AÑEJO

BACARDÍ AÑEJO CUATRO

RON DEL BARRILITO
3 STAR

IN SPANISH, "*PIÑA*" MEANS "PINEAPPLE" AND "*COLADA*" MEANS "STRAINED".

RUM PUNCH

A Rum Punch is a popular cocktail that embodies the flavours of the tropics, especially the Caribbean. The recipe can vary, but it typically includes rum or sugarcane spirit, citrus juice, a sugar, water, and sometimes additional fruit juices or spices.

HISTORY

The history of punch dates back to the 17th century, when sailors and explorers brought a mix of alcohol, citrus, sugar, and spices from India. Said to be derived from the Hindi word "*panch*", meaning "five", punch typically incorporated five key ingredients. As the British East India Company expanded trade, punch gained popularity in Europe and recipes diversified. In the Caribbean, Rum Punch blended locally produced rum with tropical flavours. The concoction thrived, evolving into a global cocktail. Today, punch varieties abound and are a testament to the history of trade, colonization, and culinary fusion.

WHAT MAKES A RUM PUNCH?

This recipe is just a starting point and many variations exist. Some might use different types of rum, add a splash of soda water, or incorporate various types of sugar or other tropical fruit juices. The key is to balance the sweetness, acidity, and the strong flavour of rum to create a refreshing beverage that captures the essence of the tropics.

LIME

GRENADINE SYRUP

HEAVY RUM

FRUIT JUICE

NUTMEG

THE RUM PUNCH THROUGH TIME

17TH CENTURY

Punch gains popularity in England. Maritime trade contributes to the spread of punch recipes, and it becomes a fashionable beverage.

18TH CENTURY

Rum becomes a common ingredient in punches as European colonizers establish sugar plantations and distilleries in the Caribbean.

20TH CENTURY

Punch remains a beloved drink, with global variations. The Caribbean Rum Punch becomes a classic cocktail.

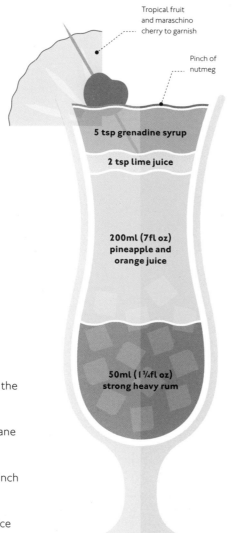

Tropical fruit
and maraschino
cherry to garnish

Pinch of
nutmeg

5 tsp grenadine syrup

2 tsp lime juice

**200ml (7fl oz)
pineapple and
orange juice**

**50ml (1¾fl oz)
strong heavy rum**

METHOD

1. Shake or build all the
ingredients with ice.

2. Pour into a hurricane
or tall glass.

3. Sprinkle over a pinch
of nutmeg.

4. Garnish with a slice
of tropical fruit and a
maraschino cherry.

WHICH RUM?

WRAY & NEPHEW OVERPROOF

**HAMPDEN ESTATE RUM
FIRE OVERPROOF**

**RIVER ANTOINE ESTATE
RIVERS ROYALE**

ONE OF SOUR, TWO OF SWEET, THREE OF
STRONG, FOUR OF WEAK, FIVE OF SPICE
TO MAKE IT NICE – THE RUM PUNCH.

TI PUNCH

The Ti Punch is often enjoyed in a leisurely manner or served as an aperitif. Its preparation is considered an art. It predates the wide availability of ice in the Caribbean, so an authentic Ti Punch is usually served without ice.

HISTORY

The Ti Punch originated in the Caribbean, particularly Martinique and Guadeloupe. More than just a drink, it's a cultural symbol in the French West Indies, deeply rooted in the traditions of the region and its connection to the production of *rhum agricole*. The ritual of making and sharing a Ti Punch brings people together. One of the unique aspects of the drink is its lack of a standardized recipe. Each drinker is encouraged to prepare their Ti Punch according to their taste, so that *chacun prépare sa propre mort* ("each one prepares their own death"). The bartender provides the glassware and ingredients, but each drinker builds their own drink.

WHAT MAKES A TI PUNCH?

A Ti Punch enhances the flavour of the sugarcane juice of *rhum agricole* with a hint of lime and sugar. Try cutting a lime disc from the edge of the fruit with the peel included. Squeezing the lime releases just a touch of juice into the glass, and adding the disc to the glass provides citrus oil.

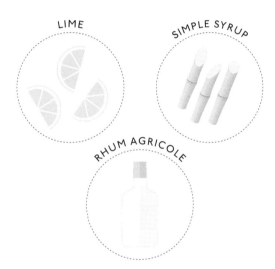

LIME

SIMPLE SYRUP

RHUM AGRICOLE

THE TI PUNCH THROUGH TIME

19TH CENTURY

Ti Punch originates in the French Caribbean, with roots dating back to the 19th century.

1890

The earliest mention of the drink was in Lafcadio Hearn's book *Two Years in the French West Indies*, where he mentions *"yon ti ponch"*.

21ST CENTURY

The use of aged *rhums agricoles* becomes more prevalent, creating a Ti Punch Vieux (Old Ti Punch).

METHOD

Note: There are no set measurements as this drink should be personal.

1. **Pour the** rhum agricole into a small rocks glass.

2. **Squeeze the** juice of a lime disc directly into the glass. You can adjust the amount of lime juice to your taste.

3. **Add simple** syrup, according to taste.

4. **Stir the** ingredients together gently. You may prefer to leave the lime disc in the glass for added flavour.

5. **Garnish with** lime zest.

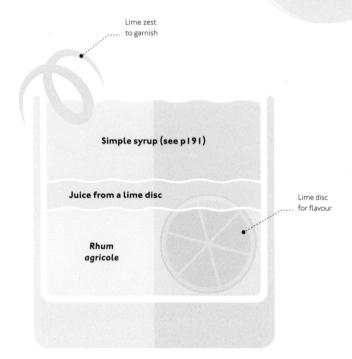

WHICH RUM?

NEISSON RHUM AGRICOLE BLANC 52.5%

LA FAVORITE COEUR DE CANNE 2 YEARS

RHUM J.M XO

Lime zest to garnish

Simple syrup (see p191)

Juice from a lime disc

Lime disc for flavour

Rhum agricole

THE NAME "TI PUNCH" IS SHORT FOR "PETIT PUNCH".

GLOSSARY

Alligator char
The heavy **charring** of the inside of oak barrels. Typically, after a prolonged burning, the barrel begins to crack and peel in a rough, shiny pattern that looks like alligator skin.

Angels' share
The portion of alcohol lost to evaporation during ageing in barrels, traditionally believed to be taken by angels. *See also* **Duppy share**.

Average age
The mean duration that the youngest and oldest rums in a blend have been aged in barrels before bottling. *See also* **Minimum age**.

Charring
The burning or toasting of the inside of an oak barrel. Rum blenders char barrels to enhance the flavour and colour of the barrel-aged rum.

Column still
Also known as a continuous still or a Coffey still, the column still consists of a tall, vertical column with multiple perforated plates or trays.

Creole still
A variant of the traditional **column still** design, often associated with French-speaking regions such as Martinique and Guadeloupe. These stills typically have modifications tailored to rum making from fresh cane juice.

Double retort pot still
A traditional distillation apparatus with two separate retorts (mini pots), allowing for multiple distillations in a single run and resulting in refined spirits with complex flavours.

Dunder
The residue or leftover material from previous distillations. Also called **stillage**, it includes the spent mash, leftover liquids, and sometimes even decomposed fruit solids.

Duppy share
A term used in Caribbean rum culture referring to the portion of rum that evaporates during ageing, believed to be taken by mischievous spirits called "duppies". *See also* **Angels' share**.

Esters
Organic compounds commonly found in fruits and flowers that contribute to their aroma and flavour. Esters are formed during fermentation when alcohols react with acids. They impart fruity, floral, and sometimes spicy notes, and play a significant role in defining the aroma and flavour profile of a rum.

Funk/funkiness
The terms "funk" and "funkiness" typically refer to a complex array of flavours and aromas that are distinctively earthy, fruity, and sometimes even pungent. This characteristic is often attributed to the unique fermentation and distillation processes used in Jamaica, particularly in traditional **pot still** distillation.

Fusel oils
Also known as fusel alcohols, a mixture of various alcohols produced as a byproduct of fermentation. They contribute to the taste and aroma of alcoholic beverages but can be undesirable in large quantities due to their strong, unpleasant odour and taste.

Heads
The volatile (low boiling point) alcohols given off at the start of distillation, such as aldehydes and ethyl acetate.

Hearts
The middle portion of the distillate, containing the desired alcohol content and flavour compounds, separated from the initial **heads** (undesirable compounds) and final **tails** (lower-quality compounds).

High wine
A distillate that has a high percentage of alcohol, but not necessarily the finished spirit. Generally, it is anything above 35% alcohol by volume (ABV).

Hogo
Derived from the French *haut gout* ("high taste"), *hogo* refers to a strong, but desirable flavour such as the slight taint of decay that is found in wild game meat. It is now

most often used to describe high-**ester** Jamaican rums.

Hybrid still

A **pot still** that combines elements of both pot and **column stills**, offering versatility in distillation methods. It typically includes a pot section for flavour and a column section for efficiency.

Low wine

The intermediate product obtained from the first distillation in **pot still** distillation. It has a lower alcohol content than the final desired product and **high wine**, and is typically redistilled to increase the alcohol concentration.

Minimum age

The length of time the youngest rum in a blend has spent ageing in an oak barrel. *See also* **Average age**.

Muck pit

In Jamaican rum making, a large outdoor fermentation pit where the molasses, cane juice, water, and natural **yeasts** are mixed and left to ferment. The muck from the pit is used to supercharge fermentation and contributes to the **funkiness** of Jamaican rum.

Pot still

A traditional distillation apparatus consisting of a large, pot-like vessel used to heat and separate alcohol from fermented liquid. Its simple design allows for the retention of flavourful compounds, resulting in rich, characterful spirits.

Rectification

The process of purifying alcohol through repeated distillation or fractional distillation. It involves separating alcohol from impurities, such as water and **fusel oils**, to create a more refined and higher-proof spirit. Rectification is crucial in producing premium-quality spirits with the desired purity, flavour, and strength.

Skimmings

The frothy layer that forms on the surface of the fermentation vat during the early stages of fermentation. It consists of various substances, including **yeast**, impurities, and proteins, which rise to the top due to their lower density.

Stripping

The initial phase of distillation where the goal is to separate (strip) alcohol, along with some water and other volatile compounds, from the **wash** quickly and efficiently using high heat to vaporize the alcohol. The vapour is then condensed back into liquid form, yielding a relatively low-proof alcohol called **low wine**.

Solera system

A method of ageing liquids, such as sherry or rum, by fractionally blending younger and older batches over time. It involves a tiered system of stacked, connected barrels, with the oldest liquid at the bottom and newer liquid added progressively from above.

Stillage

The residual material left behind after the distillation process. It typically consists of spent **wash**, **yeast**, and other byproducts of fermentation, and can be recycled for various purposes such as animal feed, fertilizer, or bioenergy products. *See also* **Dunder**.

Tails

Less volatile alcohols with higher boiling points containing **fusel oil** and little alcohol at the end of the distillation run. Also known as the "faints".

Wash

The initial liquid mixture that results from fermenting the raw ingredients used to produce rum. It typically includes water, molasses or sugarcane juice, and **yeast**. It is then distilled to create rum.

Yeast

A microorganism responsible for fermenting sugars into alcohol and carbon dioxide during the fermentation process. Different strains of yeast, such as *Schizosaccharomyces pombe* and *Saccharomyces cerevisiae*, can impart varying flavours and aromas to the final rum product.

INDEX

Page numbers in **bold** indicate main entries.

ABOUT THE AUTHOR

Ian Burrell is a global drinks personality from London of Jamaican descent. One of the most travelled figures within the beverage industry, this multi-award-winning edutainer and television drinks presenter is recognized by the rum category as the world's only global ambassador of rum. In his role as the rum ambassador, Ian travels the world educating consumers about rum's history, present, and future. He won the 2023 CLASS Bar Awards for Outstanding Contribution, and the 2024 International Wine & Spirit Competition Spirits Communicator trophy. Ian has also been voted as one of the top 10 influencers in the bar world by *Drinks International* magazine.

AUTHOR'S ACKNOWLEDGMENTS

The book in your hands would not have been possible without the dozens of people who have supported and encouraged me over the years to put some of my rum stories into print, thus sharing the knowledge to a wider audience. First and foremost, a massive thanks to the DK family, especially Cara Armstrong for commissioning the book; Izzy Holton for editorial; Vanessa Hamilton for design and illustration; Marta Bescos for hunting down the hi-res bottle shots; and Dawn Titmus, whose editing made me sound professional.

I am also hugely grateful to all the rum companies that shared rum samples, images, and information to help bring this book to life – together, we're all trying to raise the profile of the rum category, so big up to you all. To the many brands that I couldn't add to this edition, it was only due to limited space, and omitting certain brands was an arduous task.

I would also like to extend heartfelt thanks to all my rum teachers and mentors, who have been many over the years: (Aunty) Dr Joy Spence of J. Wray & Nephew; Richard Seale of Foursquare; Luca Gargano of Velier; Allen Smith and Trudiann Branker at Mount Gay Rum; Yisell Muxo and Roberto Serrallés at Destilería Serrallés; and spirit writers and friends, such as Ed Hamilton, Anistatia Miller, Jared Brown, Jeff "Beachbum" Berry, Michael Delevante, Frederick H. Smith, Ian Williams, and many more who were always there to advise and guide me as I furthered my knowledge.

There are also those who are no longer here but with me in spirit, such as Owen Tulloch, Mark Ridgwell, Tony Hart, Richard Whittingham, Laurie Barnard, George Robinson and Stephen Remsberg, Uncle Sebert, and my grandmother, who taught me how to be a great host. And, of course, I cannot forget the many enslaved Africans whom I didn't know personally but died in building the foundation of the industry that I have used to pave a way to my own freedom. They have all been instrumental in inspiring me to become a better rum ambassador and build a table of my own.

Last but not least, I want to thank my family, who, over the past several years, have had to put up with my rum travelling across the seven continents, attending countless rum festivals, and drinking cocktails in many rum bars – all in a quest to seek more rum knowledge and at the expense of our quality time together. Thank you.

Rum Love.

PUBLISHER'S ACKNOWLEDGMENTS

DK would like to thank the rum distilleries for their kind permission to reproduce images of their products, Marta Bescos for picture research, Niyran Gill for the cover illustration, John Friend for proofreading, and Vanessa Bird for the index.

PICTURE CREDITS

The publisher would like to thank the following for their kind permission to reproduce their photographs:

(Key: a-above; b-below/bottom; c-centre; f-far; l-left; r-right; t-top)

Alamy Stock Photo: 40, ARCHIVIO GBB 41, ARTGEN 50, Chronicle 39b, Chronicle 44bl, Colport 55, Eye Ubiquitous/ Paul Seheult 34, GL Archive 44bc, GRANGER – Historical Picture Archive 33, 47, Hirarchivum Press 32, JSM Historical 29, Lanmas 26, MMphotos 37t, North Wind Picture Archives 24, PBL Collection 31, Pictorial Press Ltd 37b, piemags/DCM 49t, Retro AdArchives 43, 49br, The Granger Collection 51tl, The Print Collector 58; **Bridgeman Images:** 28, Don Troiani All Rights Reserved 2024 51br, G. Dagli Orti/© NPL – DeA Picture Library 48, Leonard de Selva 38, Look and Learn 42, Manchester Art Gallery 57, Mitchell Library, State Library of New South Wales 54, Newberry Library 36; **Dreamstime.com:** Ritu Jethani 35b; **Getty Images:** Jim Heimann Collection 53, Popperfoto 45t, ZU_09 56; **Getty Images/iStock:** luoman 25; **Ian Rum Ambassador Burrell** 35t; **The Mariners' Museum, Newport News, VA:** 52.

All other images © Dorling Kindersley Limited.

DK LONDON
Editorial Director Cara Armstrong
Project Editor Izzy Holton
Senior Designer Glenda Fisher
Senior Production Editor Tony Phipps
Production Controller Celine MacLeod
Jacket Designer Glenda Fisher
Jacket Coordinator Emily Cannings
Art Director Maxine Pedliham
Publishing Director Katie Cowan

Editorial Dawn Titmus
Design and Illustration Vanessa Hamilton

First published in Great Britain in 2024 by
Dorling Kindersley Limited
DK, One Embassy Gardens, 8 Viaduct Gardens,
London, SW11 7BW

The authorized representative in the EEA is
Dorling Kindersley Verlag GmbH. Arnulfstr. 124,
80636 Munich, Germany

A CIP catalogue record for this book
is available from the British Library.
ISBN: 978-0-2416-6457-5

Printed and bound in Slovakia

www.dk.com

This book was made with Forest
Stewardship Council™ certified
paper – one small step in DK's
commitment to a sustainable future.
**Learn more at www.dk.com/uk/
information/sustainability**

Publisher's Note
DK acknowledges that the story of rum
is a multifaceted one, inextricably intertwined
with the brutal realities of colonialism and
enslavement. This book attempts to
contextualize the subject, recognizing that the
very foundations of rum production were built
upon forced labour, and including depictions of
enforced labour along with contemporary
perspectives on this fraught legacy. We aim to
acknowledge and explore these uncomfortable
truths alongside an understanding of
rum's place in our global history.